The New Art Gallery Walsall

The New Art Gallery Walsall

Batsford

Photographs 1
Hélène Binet

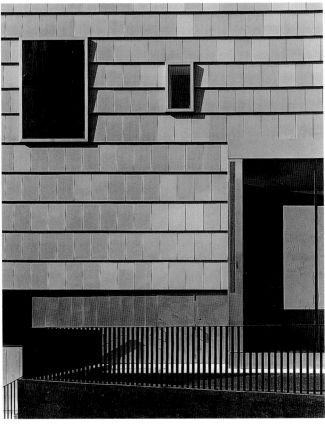

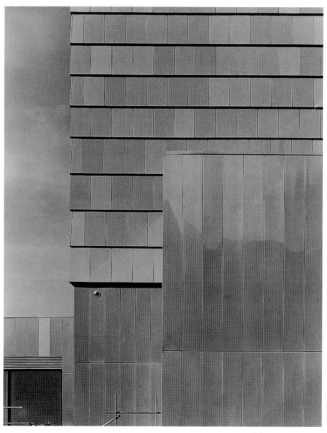

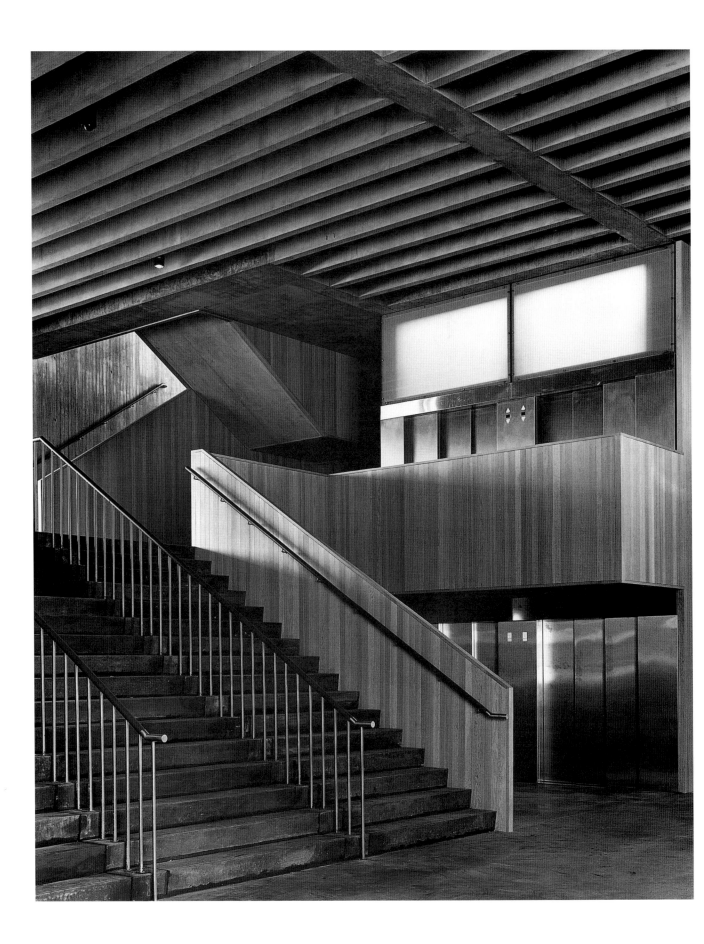

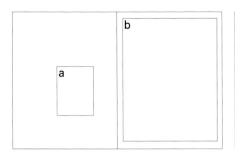

Pages 6 + 7

a From St Matthew's church
b From the west

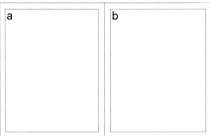

Pages 8 + 9

a From the south
b Along the canal

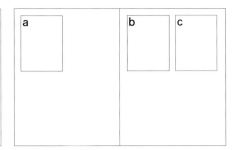

Pages 10 + 11

a From the high street
into Gallery Square
b c
The Window Box: night and day
(Town: Walsall, by Catherine Yass)

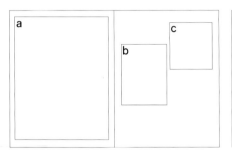

Pages 18 + 19

a Entrance hall with
stair to mezzanine
b c
Stair from mezzanine
to first floor

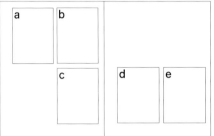

Pages 20 + 21

a Library
b Circulation space
c Restaurant
d e
Circulation space details

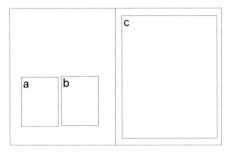

Pages 22 + 23

a b c
The Garman Ryan Collection
(first floor)

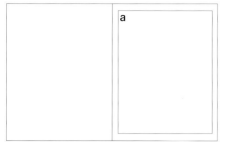

Pages 12 + 13

a Gallery entrance at night

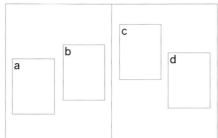

Pages 14 + 15

a Detail of south elevation
b Detail of east elevation
c Terracotta cladding with windows
d Terracotta and stainless-steel
   cladding

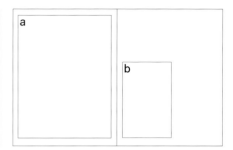

Pages 16 + 17

a The entrance foyer
b Reception

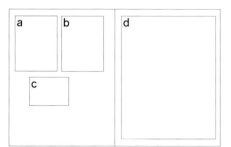

Pages 24 + 25

a b c d
Temporary exhibition spaces
(third floor)

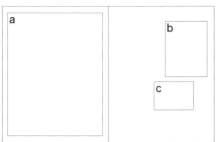

Pages 26 + 27

a The restaurant (fourth floor)
b c
   The terrace

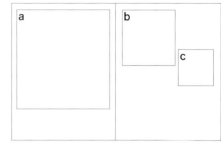

Pages 28 + 29

a b
Gallery Square,
designed by Richard Wentworth

c The canal, looking west
   from the gallery roof

Getting Under Walsall's Skin

Peter Jenkinson

The story has to start with a few words about Walsall. A predominantly industrial community of 263,000 people just north of Birmingham, located on the eastern edge of the legendarily ugly Black Country. Walsall remains a significant centre for engineering and leather-goods manufacturing.

I started work here in 1989 as Head of Museums and Galleries. As the team gradually grew, we established its reputation as being consistently lively and pioneering, exploring new ways of working with historic collections, developing exhibition, education and interpretation programmes renegotiating the complex territories of social connectedness, cultural diversity and curatorial strategies. Underpinning all this was a philosophy that stresses the central and critical role that local people play in the representation and questioning of culture and cultures.

While the 'art world' was slow to understand this philosophy and some of our work was unfunded for many years, the audience at our gallery grew to be one of the most diverse and active in the country.

After ten years in the planning and three long and hard years of construction, The New Art Gallery opened its automatic doors to the public on 16 February 2000 and at that moment our dreams became reality. A few days later staff were looking back nostalgically to the days before visitors arrived, dropping rubbish, leaving marks, asking questions, complaining, touching the art, losing an unbelievable assortment of objects. And yet of course, without the visitors and their demands and concerns it would not be an art gallery. We were simultaneously enthused, exhilarated, elated and deeply moved by the range as well as the number of people who flocked through the doors. This hot and messy scrum of visitors experiencing the building, but also experiencing each other's presence in free public space, is exactly what we imagined when we set out to plan a gallery that would be unapologetically world-class yet accessible to all, a democratic space of the highest quality and a focus for community life.

From its inception, the brief for the Gallery was that it should represent excellence – the very best in terms of art, architecture and public space, rejecting the sad British tradition of cutting corners, compromising, of making do and getting by in public projects. Equally, we wanted the gallery to be a model of accessibility, enabling people from across the social spectrum to engage with and participate in the arts, making strong long-term relationships between audiences, art, artists and children. Also from its inception, admission to the Gallery was planned proudly and passionately to be free. We set out to prove that the belief that excellence and access were mutually incompatible was false, a cynical prejudice.

Starting with a derelict site – a muddy unsurfaced car park – at the top of Walsall's main shopping street, a series of complicated processes began. These involved massive public consultation, the slow building of political and community consensus, the engagement of support from national agencies and from individuals, masterplanning and refining the brief and then, in 1995, an international architecture ideas competition. The intention was not to find a final design but an architectural practice that the gallery team could work with. We wanted the competition to make a space for young and less-known practices. It was a fantastic experience that allowed extraordinary conversations about what a gallery for the twenty-first century might be.

From 73 entrants from all over Europe, we selected six practices. Among them was muf, the artist and architect collaborative. They proposed a gallery with a 24-hour bar/café, a tattoo parlour, a launderette and artist allotments on the roof. You would be able to come along, throw your laundry into a washing machine, see a show, meet a friend for a coffee, or tend to the gardening.

In the end we chose the London-based practice Caruso St John. They had not designed a gallery before and their largest completed building at that time cost £500,000. It was some kind of leap of faith to award them a contract for a £21 million art gallery but we were totally persuaded by their ideas, their responsiveness to the brief, to Walsall and to the rehousing of the Garman Ryan Collection. They were passionate and could talk intelligently about art, especially contemporary art.

They proposed a tall gallery of many different spaces, describing it as being like a big house to be explored and discovered by visitors as they moved between the floors. It would be a gallery with many windows varying in scale from the domestic to the cinemascopic, flooding the gallery with light but also, and critically, allowing views out of the gallery to the town and the region beyond. Many of the architects in the competition had been sniffy about a gallery located next to Woolworths and Bhs and proposed schemes that turned their back on this retail reality. Like us, Caruso St John celebrated the fact that you could pop in to both store and gallery for a bit of pick 'n' mix and that the gallery could be a part of everyday life, connected and real.

After five years of work, the result is a 37-metre-high tower clad in pale terracotta tiles, punctuated by many windows that hang like picture frames on the terracotta. Inside, visitors start at a generous reception space and explore a building of astonishing quality, built to last.

More than five thousand people of all ages and from all backgrounds toured the site during construction. Schools were involved in hundreds of projects – writing, dance and drama. Talks, tours, workshops, artists' commissions, competitions – during the launch period this energetic public involvement was continued with artists and schools making shop-window displays in twenty stores while buses brought people from outlying areas to the gallery with linked discounts in local shops. While all these events and happenings had been planned by the gallery, what has amazed us is that people of all kinds are requesting to use the place for their own purposes – jazz and symphony concerts, club nights, dance performances, fashion shows, opera, press conferences, abseiling events for charity, fire brigade emergency training. And people use it in the ways visitors have always used galleries: as a meeting place, a place to show off, as a pick-up joint. The gallery is being used as a civic building, full of community life and aspiration and communication.

In fact, the building is performing almost like a town in its own right, with the citizens visibly exercising their right to participate in the life of the community and in the story of art and architecture. I don't know why this celebration of civic space should be happening now but I think it has something to do with the disappearing public realm, the fact that we have gone through a profoundly anti-democratic period with increasing privatisation and control of public space, the ghettoisation of communities and their experiences, a prime minister who said that there is no such thing as society. But there is, and people want to be part of it.

For generations the people of Walsall have been expected to accept second or third best. They know what quality is, but they have also learnt not to ask for too much for fear of disappointment. The most powerful justification of every penny of the £21 million that has been spent on the creation of The New Art Gallery Walsall is the powerful impact it has had on the hearts and minds of local people.

Essays

The New Art Gallery and its geography

Irénée Scalbert

Few towns have been so completely shaped by work as Walsall has. Streets and yards, buildings and vacant lots all bear the marks of relentless labour. The signs of ingenuity and effort, of production and waste, of wealth and deprivation are visible everywhere, in no particular order. For two centuries, land in Walsall has been a source of raw materials and the place to work them. For this reason, the town is a mess. Nikolaus Pevsner, a historian who might be expected to have known, thought so.[1] Looking across the canal from the west, weather-beaten sheds and the cinder-like remains of factories lie between obsolete chimneys. *(ill.1)* Beyond, there stand in slow succession a 1960s office block, The New Art Gallery, the tower of the Edwardian town hall (disquietingly small), a dense cluster of multi-storey housing blocks and, last and some distance away, the parish church of St Matthew.

The view betrays little about the plan or the state of Walsall, save that it must be partly incoherent and derelict. Unrelated on the skyline except through mere coincidence, the industrial, commercial, civic and domestic buildings are connected from the base. By the canal they stand, as if on a plinth of long brick walls, pallisades and galvanised railings, on

land which for centuries has been a waste leased for every purpose except agriculture. The new gallery is squat and flat, with moments of brightness when the stainless steel of its crest catches the afternoon sun. Not in the least conspicuous, it is merely one of them, a building among others, all equally laconic and plain.

The only landmark in this uncommunicative, treeless landscape is the hill upon which St Matthew's stands. Moving across the fractured field, likened by Caruso St John to a Cézanne, to this blunt Mont St Victoire, now looking back from the steps descending from the church, another view presents itself which contradicts in almost every aspect what has so far been described. *(ill.2)* At the bottom of the stairs, across the road, large brick planters keep cars out of the high street. To the left, the polycarbonate vault of a shopping arcade sets the tone for most commercial precincts in the town centre. Facing it to the right, the old Guildhall, built in the thick-set Baroque favoured by Victorians, now hosts a pizzeria. Looking down the high street, its space, the market stalls and the crowd dominate the view, while in the distance, seemingly on axis with the street, The New Art Gallery appears to close the view.

1   Nikolaus Pevsner;
     *The Buildings of England:
     Staffordshire;*
     London, 1974

ill 1 Photograph Hélène Binet
ill 2 Photograph Hélène Binet

Its scale is large, and the building can be clearly made out in the morning light. A tower rises asymmetrically above the main volume of the building, in the manner of the Palazzo Vecchio in Florence. Its centre is clearly marked by a large square opening, but it is undermined below by a sequence of three windows which run to the nearest corner. Thus the gallery appears to be tottering around the vertical, and to edge to the right toward the true centre of the high street. As one walks into town, the silhouette of the building soon becomes lost in the crowd. Further down, it reappears, head and one shoulder above the buildings which form the side of Digbeth Street and, later, Park Street, and vanishes again. But the gesture is not forgotten. It secures a connection between the gallery and the oldest public space of the town, its high street. It claims a bond between the high-minded purpose of the new building and the people of Walsall 'going down the town' on market days, to borrow an evocative local expression.

The two views could hardly be more contrasted. From the west, a vision of entropy appears to capture the entire pathology of Britain. It is broad and panoramic, and no single feature appears more meaningful than another. It presents the image of a town where nothing adds up, without plan, impenetrable and inhospitable to life. Repeatedly subjected to development, little is left but the ruins of building, the cavities of mining and the waste. Not at all the place of historical sedimentation which, still today, typifies urban imagination, this is the place, literally, of rabid extraction. This town is as good as what can be got from it.

From the east, the view is narrow, highly focussed and crowded. If the whole of Walsall were to be laid waste for profit, the integrity of the main street, one feels, would survive with its distinctive topography, with its high street tumbling down the hill, with the double bend leading into Digbeth, the level square at the 'Bridge' beneath which the River Tame has long been culverted, and the gentle rise of Park Street beyond, which fans out in front of Woolworths, a few metres short of The New Art Gallery. Unaffected by the industrial revolution, impervious to the quick succession of shopping developments, resistant to all attempts at gentrification by paving and by design, the endurance of this space is mysterious and deeply affecting. It is the definitive monument to the resilience of a people who continue 'going down the town'.

The early plan of Walsall has been compared to a human figure, its head resting on the hillside of St Matthew's, its arms branching out at the Bridge and its feet lying at the end of Park Street. For centuries this body was laid in open fields and meadows if not, still earlier, in the forest of Cannock. Today, it is spread in a half-industrialised, half-urbanised landscape, but the simile retains its force. The new gallery stands at the feet of this figure, on a site aptly known as Town End where Park Street forks out into lesser roads leading into the Black Country. Here it articulates the transition between the public character of the high street and the emptiness of the waste, St Matthew's on the hill and stand-alone factories in the plain, between figurative expression and terse objectivity, between morning vista and afternoon panorama. This position can seem fortuitous, revealing no more than a banal contrast between a town centre and its periphery. But there exists in Walsall underlying reasons which confer the character of necessity on this confrontation, and therefore on the gallery and its site. Here, as in few other places to the same degree, these reasons lie in its geology.

The centre of Walsall stands on an island of marine deposits sharply faulted to the north and to the south. *(ill.3)* Like the Dudley hills a few miles to the west, it is built on some of the oldest ground in the country, on an outpost of the Pennine ridges in the Welsh borderlands. Formed

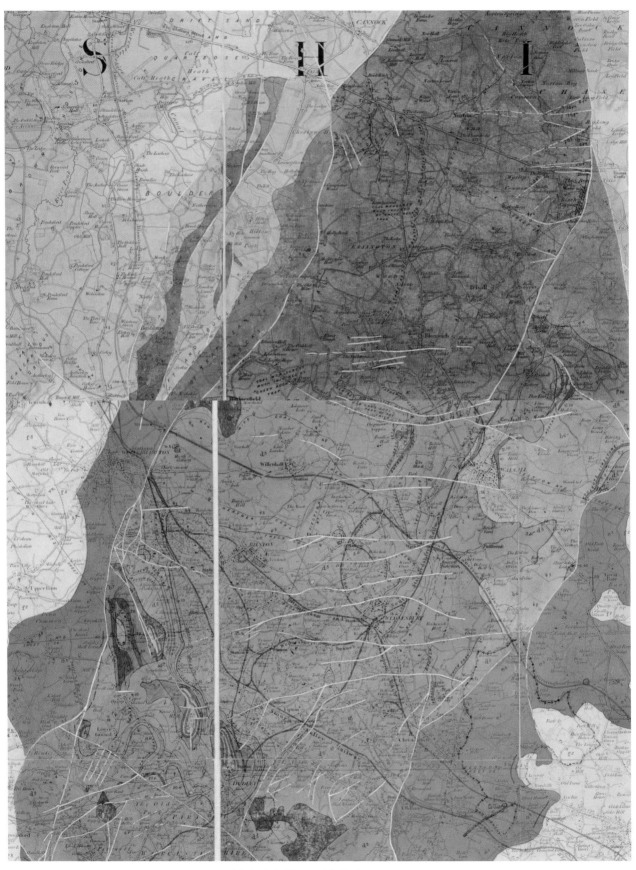

ill 3 Geological Survey of England,
1855, British Library. Walsall is
in the centre right of the map,
in the mauve section

some four hundred million years ago, the grey mudstones and shales rise gently together with the High Street. Two long outcrops of Wenlock limestone run across this ground, closing as it were both ends of the street. One of them skirts the hill behind St Matthew's, and terminates at the Arboretum where it was once extensively mined. The other runs across Town End and it is here that The New Art Gallery now stands. Some hundred metres at most to the west, the inclined strata of this ancient island slip beneath the coal measures, to the bottom of the carboniferous basin.

A hundred million years passed. River-borne silts which the weaker currents failed to carry seaward were deposited along the limestone shores. In the lower parts of the coal measures, seams of shales, clays and sandstones, of coal and ironstones bear witness to the complexity of their formation. These strata were intensely folded, plicated and fractured in a network of faults as closely jammed together as the lines on the palm of a hand. They formed at first a hilly and possibly mountainous terrain, until their rugged surface became levelled by dry weathering and torrential rains. At last red sandstones and marls were thrown in ample folds over the greater part of the county, leaving the carboniferous basin rimmed by the Triassic plain.

Today, The New Art Gallery stands like a beacon on the shore, surrounded on three sides by this great lake of coal and melancholy. From its terrace, the entire coalfield of South Staffordshire can be embraced, six miles across and twenty three miles long. Here men have mined coal, clay and ironstone. Here they built railways and factories, they erected whole towns which stand on a ground repeatedly disturbed and now so tired that it has long been prone to subsidence. Intense activity broke out at the dawn of the nineteenth century, then redoubled around 1850 in a prodigious display of resourcefulness and collective willpower. By then, Britain was known as the workshop of the world. The Black Country and the towns which grew along its perimeter, notably Birmingham, Wolverhampton and Walsall, were the great manufacturing centres of the country. Here people made their extraordinary contribution to the Industrial Revolution, the significance of which recent developments in Korea, China and South-East Asia are unlikely to undermine or surpass.

An Industrial Landscape

The revolution was no more predictable than the fires that ignited spontaneously in the depths of the coalfield, as in Wednesbury to the south-west of Walsall where some eleven acres were smouldering uncontrollably in the late seventeenth century. The early introduction of coke and steam power in furnaces encouraged the proliferation of mines, forges, foundries, naileries and other workshops from Wolverhampton to Walsall. The construction of the canal system which reached Town End in the late eighteenth century acted as a catalyst for the coal industry. The production of pig iron was boosted by the Napoleonic wars, and again in the 1860s by the construction of railways, which in turn opened the London market for Staffordshire coal. All these were milestones in making revolutionary change the norm.

Yet one factor contributed more than any other in determining the actual form of the landscape: in no other place in Britain was there such an abundance of coal lying so close to the surface. As a result, mining on a large scale started early in the Black Country, and a pattern was set for the extraction of coal, characterised by small, primitive and wasteful undertakings. A first generation of operators took the pickings where they were easily accessible. Others worked over the uncharted field again and again, until mines were seldom more than three hundred metres apart. With no consistent drainage policy, they became water-logged. Soon, the four hundred collieries in the exposed coalfield were no longer viable or simply exhausted. By 1920, all had closed, and mining activity moved to a few large, deep winnings in the borders of the field.

It is often assumed that Walsall, being on the edge of the Black Country, was chiefly occupied if not in mining, then in iron smelting. But in a town with up to eighty thousand inhabitants in the 1880s, the entire borough contained just six furnaces. Instead, development which, in the words used in the first and only guide book to Walsall (published in 1889), was 'truly marvellous',[2] favoured industries like smitheries and bit-making. These grew from the requirements of horse transport (as important then as car transport is today) and it is in bit-making in particular that the extraordinary industrial diversity of Walsall, dubbed 'the town with a thousand trades', could be most clearly appreciated.

The stirrup trade for example, in which the town had de facto a country-wide monopoly, was so finely tuned to the market as to produce bits 'with India rubber mouths for sensitive horses, as well as such as are required for the most powerful and restive animals'.[3] Many products were made for export, from camel spurs to 'spurs of a peculiar make for South America'.[4] Others were the tools needed by the casters, forgers, filers and finishers who together constituted the bit-making industry, as well as saddlers and harness makers. Every kind of chain could be found, even those for dogs, monkeys and parrots. So could electrical fittings and instruments including 'philosophical, telephonic, phonographic, medical and experimental apparatus and appliances'.[5]

By the end of the nineteenth century, products made in Walsall were exported to every part of the world and raw materials were imported from as many parts to Walsall. In brush-making for example, in the piles of materials awaiting to be turned by a single firm into '5000 kinds of brooms and brushes of various sizes

and shapes, from the large unwieldy gun brush for cleaning cannon to the tiniest camel-hair pencil for the artist's use', there could be found 'bristles of all colours and qualities from Germany, Russia, Siberia, China, India and America; fibres from Mexico, Ceylon, and South Africa; weeds from Italy and South America, beautifully dressed horse and camel hair, and carefully prepared whale bone'.[6] Nothing was too remote for import or too special for manufacture.

In 'the race of intelligent progress',[7] intelligence was gathered in the work place. Gradually, the need for independent centres of knowledge became felt. In 1831, when the town was fifteen thousand strong, a first library was opened and served principally middle-class subscribers. Ten years later, it was renamed the Walsall Literary and Philosophical Institution, suggesting a growing ambition that was legitimised by the visits of, inter alia, Oscar Wilde and Prince Kropotkin. In addition to lectures, the institution included, until its closure in 1875, the first museum in the town and a laboratory whose purpose is unlikely to have been conservation. In the 1850s, the population had almost doubled, reaching forty thousand at the end of the decade. The expansion took place chiefly in the suburbs, for example in Bloxwich where new collieries were being opened, and it coincided with the massive industrialisation which was under way in many parts of Britain. In this period, the first public library (and one of the first in the country) was inaugurated, and free lectures were soon introduced for working men.

In the 1880s Sunday morning adult schools were founded. One of them, the Artisans' Art Class, was located four hundred metres away from the site of The New Art Gallery, in a back yard off Bridgeman Street. Its premises were hemmed in between narrow cottages, a Methodist chapel, a harness furniture manufactory, an inn and a chain manufactory. *(ill.4)* After this humble

2   W. Henry Robinson;
     Guide to Walsall, 1889
3   Op. cit. note 2
4   Op. cit. note 2
5   Op. cit. note 2
6   Op. cit. note 2
7   Op. cit. note 2

ill 4 Walsall in the 1880s
X   site of The New Art Gallery
O   site of Science and Art Institute
V   St Matthew's Church

45

Walsall Canal

New Art Gallery

Woolworths

Bhs

town wharf
phase 1

Superdrug

Boots

Rail Station

Marks & Spencer

Littlewoods

The Saddlers
Centre

McDonalds

John Menzies

WH Smith

Mothercare

Bus Station

Next

Etam

Burton

Virgin

Dixons

ill 5 View of the high street and
Town End from the east, from a
brochure issued by Chartwell
Land plc

town wharf
phase 2

Walsall
College of
Technology

Multi-storey
Car Park
390

47

beginning, the Art Class was amalgamated with the Science Institution, and the Science and Art Institute was created. New premises were built in Bradford Place in 1888, between a railway shed and a stone yard, and, abutting at the rear, the largest currying works in the town 'and in the world'.[8] *(ill.5)* No less than sixteen hundred students enrolled in its first session, in classes which included many branches of science, the fine arts, literature, and music, as well as leather tanning, metallurgy, carpentry and joinery, steam and the steam engine, and shorthand. The handsome red brick neo-gothic building still exists. It now hosts a school for painters and decorators with, in its great hall, a surreal display of old-fashioned shop signs and cubicles for painting practice.

The eclectic range of courses offered by these proud institutions bears witness to a remarkable curiosity. In the race for intelligent progress, there was no time for the fine distinctions, now taken for granted and carefully maintained, between education, aesthetic appreciation and recreation. A speech delivered in 1892 by the then President of the Chamber of Commerce illustrates the spontaneous association between knowledge, beauty and pleasure.[9] The occasion was the opening of Walsall's first public art gallery on the upper floor of the Free Library, with displays of paintings, crafts from the Kensington Museum in London, New Guinea curiosities, fossils, birds' eggs and other miscellany. The President pointed to the art on the walls and, to the delight of his audience, to how abominable the gearing was on the magnificent horses that had been painted. If only, he said, with the help of the students at the Science and Art Institute, these animals had been harnessed with goods manufactured in Walsall, they could attract visitors to the town from all parts of the country.

The Garman Ryan Collection

A hundred years have passed, and the town's goods do not attract as many visitors as they did in the past. But its art still might. In 1972 Walsall was fortunate in being offered works assembled by Kathleen Garman and Sally Ryan, all of which are now housed in The New Art Gallery. The collection includes portraits of the collectors' relatives which give to the collection an intimate, near biographical character. The diversity of media - drawings, watercolours, etchings, oils and sculptures are all represented - and the small scale of the works, many of them studies, make them particularly suitable for teaching. The presence of Jacob Epstein, partner of Kathleen Garman, the teacher of Sally Ryan and the greatest sculptor working in Britain in the first half of the twentieth century, can be felt throughout the collection. Thus, if the vocation of the art gallery is no longer, in the words of the late President of the Chamber of Commerce, 'to amuse and make happier the most humble member of the community' and to make the manners of the people 'softer and less uncouth than they were [sic] at present',[10] the Garman Ryan Collection can still please, instruct and move.

The thematic arrangement of works demanded by Kathleen Garman, including for example children, trees, animals and flowers, makes the collection immediately accessible, thus fulfilling an essential objective of The New Art Gallery. Its spontaneous, homely character, more striking perhaps than the overall Modernist sensibility which presided over its assembly, establishes a distant link with the collections displayed in Walsall a century earlier. By coincidence, like its forerunner, the Garman Ryan Collection includes objects from New Guinea, presented to our more demanding though less inquiring minds as works of art wanting our admiration rather than as curiosities appealing to our understanding.

Science and Art Institute, Walsall.

8   Op.cit. note 2
9   *Walsall Observer*, May 21
     1892; kindly supplied to
     the author by The New
     Art Gallery

10   Op.cit. note 9

ill.6 Walsall's Science and
Art Institute, 1888

Developing Town Wharf

Walsall ranks among the poorest local-authority districts in Britain in the index of deprivation compiled by the government, where it is preceded notably by Birmingham and most London inner-city boroughs. It fares badly in education where aspirations are low, and it has more derelict land than most districts in the country. One of the worst affected areas is that of Town End. (ill.6) A hundred years ago, it was densely built up with houses, workshops, factories, wharves and mining facilities. Most of these buildings have been demolished. Today industrial sheds stand in the Town Wharf Business Park, to the south of the canal. To the north, pending an imminent 170,000-square-foot retail development, there is little else but waste land and temporary car-parks. To most except its inhabitants, Walsall has become a typical post-industrial town, even though close to half its working population is employed, still, in manufacturing industries.

For more than a century, the caverns of disused limestone quarries had been supported by monolithic pillars and made much of the ground in Town End unsafe for construction. In the late 1980s, ash from power stations mixed with cement was pumped into them, thus clearing the way for redevelopment. The area was close to the town centre and to the motorway. The canal provided an amenity upon whose value everyone could agree and enabled Town End to metamorphose into Town Wharf. In the early 1990s, the municipality commissioned a feasibility study for the area. Perspective drawings rehearsed familiar scenes, most of them Mediterranean in character, in keeping with the urban design which has prevailed since the war. A sketch plan showed two stores closing the end of Park Street where they formed a public space complete with a 'focal feature' – clock, sundial, statue or fountain. A passage led between them into a new square beyond, flanked on two sides by the back walls of the same stores, and defined on a third by a pub and the canal basin.

This study, in which the provision of a new gallery for the Garman Ryan Collection was first envisaged in Town End, formed the basis for a successful application for City Challenge funding. In 1992 Walsall was awarded £35 million by the central government, of which £4 million were allocated to the Town Wharf area. Land was acquired, the bus station was moved, services were installed and the canal dredged. Once the area between Park Street and the canal had been prepared, a developer could be appointed, and the two stores, leased to Woolworths and Bhs, were built at the end of Park Street between 1994 and 1996. Profits from the successful commercial operation were capped and the proceeds to the municipality secured the purchase of land for the new gallery. In addition, the developer, Chartwell, financed the construction of the pub on the new square and sponsored the international architectural competition for the gallery, launched in July 1995.

The site was not promising. It was cut off from Park Street and the main public space of the town. The canal had not been dredged and most buildings alongside it were derelict. The elevations supplied in the brief for the Woolworths and Bhs stores gave no hint of local architecture patronage. From the top of a pile of rubble standing on the site, St Matthew's was clearly visible beyond the vacant lots where the stores were still to be built. This suggested to Caruso St John that a direct visual connection between the new gallery and the parish church might be established. In this town where everything that was good – industry, wealth, learning and urbanity – appeared to be vanishing, the new building was going to be tall and civic in character.

The competition brief, illustrated with pictures of local children, conveyed the enthusiasm of Peter Jenkinson, the Director of Museums and Galleries in Walsall, and his commitment to education

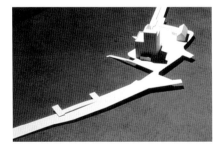

and to achieving a high public profile for the gallery. Thus the tone of the project was set right at the beginning, before architects and client had even met: it embraced at once the architects' implicit protest at the town's neglect and the client's belief in the value of education and openness.

Between Warehouse and Arthouse

The three A1 boards submitted by the architects for the first stage of the competition have been lost. Only a card model of the site and a few photographs of another, showing a tentative section through the building, survive. These last indicate five storeys of equal height connected by stairs which, rather than being regularly stacked one above the other, rose in different places within the floors. *(ill.7)* Pieces of corrugated cardboard were inserted, suggesting intimate, house-like spaces embedded in the more generalised space of a warehouse-like structure. The arrangement drew from Kettle's Yard in Cambridge which remained a point of reference throughout the design. Adolf Loos's raumplan in the Villa Müller in Prague was another immediate source - even though the plan of another building, that of an Arts & Crafts house from Sweden, featured on a presentation board.

The model was faced with sacking, masking the interior behind a semi-transparent curtain wall. *(ill.8)* The functional distribution of the building was barely touched upon. A section in mere outline included the names of the most important spaces - café, exhibition, Garman Ryan, terrace, restaurant, etc. - and hinted at a possible vertical sequence. The squat proportions of the volume, the mesh-like screen of its elevations, the serial arrangement of floors suggesting autonomy and variety: all drew from the same source, OMA's celebrated ZKM project for the city of Karlsruhe.

The site model, complete with access ramp to the railway station, reflects the extent of the architects' knowledge of the town obtained during a first visit to Walsall. *(ill.9)* It betrays their lack of enthusiasm for the commercial architecture (much of it from the 1970s) along the sides of the high street, which has been neatly omitted. In turn it conveys the importance ascribed to the ground as a public, connecting, smooth element which prefigures Richard Wentworth's design adopted for the square a year later (bar the stripes). At this early stage, the position of roads on the site had not been decided. Like other buildings in the vicinity, the lock keeper's cottage by the side of the canal was derelict. The architects did not like the shape proposed by British Waterways for the new basin, designed to accomodate the turning circles of barges and to align with the sides of the new stores. On all sides they were faced with prospects which were either undecided or dismal.

Only the canal seemed permanent, and it seems therefore natural to position the new tower on its axis. In the second stage of the competition, the architects gambled on the redrawing of the basin. They aligned its long sides with the axis of the canal and gave it dimensions which reflect those of the gallery facade above. Alongside it to the north, the pub fronted the new square with a gable end. Thus both the axis of the canal and that of Park Street were closed, the first by the full stop of the gallery, the second by the comma of the pub.

Moreover, the placing of these two buildings helped to establish a relation of equivalence between the basin and the square. In this way, the problem of the articulation between the canal and Park Street was solved through its replay on the site itself. The two axes were allowed to slide past one another and were brought into relation by a series of diagonal, informal stitches: from basin to square, from pub to gallery, from gallery entrance to Park Street, and from waste land to town centre. Axial or local symmetries are replaced, according to

ill 7 First stage model. Section
ill 8 Model: interior masked behind a semi transparent curtain wall
ill 9 Site model

St John, with 'organic frontalities', the entrance of the gallery for example dominating the entire square even though it is aligned with no element within it. Beyond the area of the model, two buildings remained impressed in the architects' mind: the parish church of St Matthew which suggested the tower, and the factory rising at the end of Station Road to the south. Their images were projected in the design and became 'figures' or 'gestures', two notions often referred to by Caruso and St John. From the church, a generic sense of relationship to the surroundings was retained. As you turn the corner by Bhs and Woolworths, The New Art Gallery looms improbably close to them, reminding St John of how Chartres cathedral suddenly appears at the end of the small surrounding streets. Coming from the opposite side, from the canal, it appears to push against the back of the stores to make space for the basin and to assert its presence on the high street. From afar, the gallery provides a high point to a cluster of buildings which seem more tightly packed than they are in reality. Hung inside the tower of the building, chandeliers can be clearly made out from a distance in the tall 'church-like' space of the restaurant, like bells.

The factory, described by the architects as 'very sheer, very clean ... very confident and right', contributed architectural rather than urban qualities. It shares with the gallery the precision, the lack of affectation in the details which one expects in the workplaces of the Midlands. Its conspicuous water tower, positioned asymmetrically above the main volume of the building, painted black with 'BOAK' painted in tall white letters on its four sides (*ill 10*), triggered the process of modelling which has made the profile of the gallery at least equally distinctive and memorable. Like the influence and counter influence of the canal and the high street on the site plan, the impressions left by the factory and by the church played against one another. They were gradually absorbed in the design and helped to emphasisze

ill 10 The BOAK building

the shifts of mood which occur throughout the building between factual and expressive qualities, between warehouse and Art House.

First Impressions

In the first stage of the competition, the cut-out of the entrance already undermined the building at its most prominent edge, where it is tallest. In the second stage, in September and October 1995, it was made larger still. Two single-storey volumes projecting out at the base of the building locked the volume of the gallery to the shape of the site. The first, a café, reached westwards almost to the edge of the basin. The other, the bookshop, was adjacent to the entrance and wrapped around the eastern corner of the ground floor. Subsequently, a display window for art replaced the shop (which was too small), and the shop was combined with the café.

Once past the entrance, the entire lobby is visible at a glance. Vast in its dimensions, it appears larger still because it is approached diagonally. The eye is first drawn to the main stairs. Other spaces are soon noticed, scattered on a broad panoramic arc: the discovery gallery which forms the lower level of a three-storey 'children's house', the library on the mezzanine, the lifts, the bookshop, and last and tucked to the side, an information desk dwarfed by so much space and so vast an acreage of concrete.

The client brief stressed that 'first impressions matter'. Here they do in a manner which outreaches the previsions of the architects. Orientation is easy, the several uses along the perimeter promise liveliness, and the space as a whole conveys a sublime grandeur. Yet this space is more than grand. It is huge, sombre in tone and cavernous in a way the plan submitted for the competition, then almost wholly open to the square on the north side, did not anticipate. Its seven-metre clearance is spectacular, and its concrete structure is so plainly manifested that one does feel, not without a tremor, the entire weight of the building resting on the precast beams overhead. As often in the tradition of civic architecture, the experience of grandeur entails both a display of largesse and a rite of passage.

The broad flights reach to the mezzanine, past the proscenium-like timber-clad walls on either side. Beyond the landing, the stairs are reduced in width, they turn back on themselves and exit to the first floor in a pirouette, as if to confirm that the civic display had been staged for effect. This after all is a multi-storey building serviced by lifts, precluding from the outset a sense of hierarchy between floors.

A proper gesture
From the first floor onwards, the lifts rise behind the face of the building on axis with the canal. They are glazed and the view is interrupted at regular intervals by the concrete beams bracing the building. Coming out of the lift on the upper floor, one finds oneself on the reverse side, as it were, of the proscenium wall, in a space where the entire view is revealed at once. Wind bars mark the south and east sides of the winter garden, beyond which lies the terrace. They are slender and plain, and it is not the bars but the landscape, shallow and infinitely delicate like froth sitting above the parapet, which one notices first.

Walking the length of this space, picking here the spire of St Matthew's, there the tower of the town hall, a broad, low timber-lined passage to the left leads to the restaurant. Here, in a building which deliberately spurns the art of sequence, is a space described by the architects as the 'grand finale', the fermata. Beyond the close ranks of tables, five large openings file round the corner of the room, held down to the floor by the timber dado of which they are (but only just) a part. They are so large that everything behind the glass, for example the 1960s tower block planted at the end of Park Street, dubbed by St John a 'little piece from New York',

appears close enough to touch. Looking east, the eye skims along the high street, all the way to St Matthew's. Looking up into the tower, the space rises high above the dado, where there is scarcely anything but concrete. Two windows of similar size push against the coffered beams of the ceiling and face each other across the void as if to give pause to think. From viewing into thinking, from bare facts into gesture, the transformation now seems familiar.

Yet the architects were working over a scheme which had been determined by other factors. In the early sectional model, the room within the tower was given a height equal to that of other floors in the building. *(ill.7)* The sides of the terrace rose to the same height, thus creating a room without a roof, like a space by the artist James Turrell. But this contributed awkward proportions to the east elevation: the body of the building seemed hunched and its head sunken. The architects lowered the enclosure of the terrace to parapet height. The building now terminates at three rather than two separate levels, its profile at its most emphatic where the lowest and highest levels meet on the east façade. The gallery no longer merely winks with a window or nods with a tower, but makes a proper gesture which the architects liken in jest to the Modular Man of Le Corbusier and to the Statue of Liberty facing out into the Atlantic.

Little big building
The building accommodates as many floors as there were main items in the brief, namely the entrance hall, the Garman Ryan Collection, the temporary exhibition galleries and, to use a crude Manhattanism, the penthouse. In the early stages of the design, the top-floor restaurant excepted, the height and size of rooms, like the height of the tiles on the outside, decreased as one ascended in the building. After the competition, the most significant change demanded by Peter Jenkinson was to reverse the order between temporary exhibitions and permanent collections. The two Garman

Ryan floors became in a double sense the centre of gravity of the building. They are situated immediately above the entrance hall to be accessed more easily and visited more often. Moreover their layout, consisting of small rooms arranged on two storeys, forms a structural 'net' which carries, quite literally, the entire weight of the building to the perimeter walls (a further legacy of the ZKM project and its Vierendeel truss structure) and leaves the entrance hall on the ground floor column-free and undivided.

As a result, the clerestory windows of the temporary exhibition spaces were relocated closer to the top of the building, forming on the outside a nearly continuous frosted architrave, fluorescent and garishly green after dusk. The long stairs were introduced. They provide an alternative route to the now separate circulation within the Garman Ryan spaces, and were replicated between the two upper floors. Narrow and in places immensely tall, they are monumental, but one remains surprisingly unaware of their presence, like the stairs concealed within the wall thickness of medieval castles.

The ubiquitous precast concrete beams are more deliberately medieval in character. On the temporary exhibition floor, they create a powerful effect, compared by Caruso with the beamed ceilings of the state rooms in the Papal Palace at Avignon. On the Garman Ryan floors, medieval traces remain in the two-storey hall around which all the rooms are gathered, and in the adjacent corridor, compared to a long gallery, which leads to it. At a glance, the plan suggests a neo-classical layout with rooms en enfilade, routinely adopted for new galleries during the last twenty years. But rather than leading axially from one room to the next, connections are made in the corners and circulation lead outward to the perimeter of the building and the light, and inward to the hall and the warmth of its timber cladding.

Even in the Garman Ryan Collection, spaces are generous in size and affecting in their material presence. But the building as a whole feels small. The architects wanted a 'tower' to make the building visible in the town, and a 'house' to give a domestic character to its spaces. What they achieved is more particular. They created a big tower which feels small like a house, and a house whose spaces feel big like those inside a tower. This play between the very small and the very large, between actual size and figural scale distinguishes many public buildings, for instance cathedrals, which combine, like the gallery, a teeming of architectural details and a sense of disproportion. Medieval allusions recur throughout. Indeed The New Art Gallery appears to prefigure a medieval revival, set against Modernism and corporate capitalism. It echoes the Art and Science Institute, itself a plain example of the Gothic Revival defined a century earlier in opposition to neo-classicism and industrialization.

A moralised landscape

The scatter of windows on the façade was among the first ideas adopted by the architects during the second stage of the competition. It hints at the range of spaces within, and it maintains the veil-like effect of the initial, ZKM-like proposal. But the scale of the windows relative to the overall volume of the gallery was too brutal and required mediation. Hence tiles were introduced, giving the building a strong three-dimensional texture within which the random pattern formed by the windows could be effectively absorbed. At first, it was envisaged that they be made in pigmented concrete, silk-screened in places with images of Epstein's sculptures in a 'fit of homage' to Herzog & de Meuron. The specification was later upgraded to terracotta, a material often used on Victorian buildings and which seemed appropriate in Walsall. Moreover the density of terracotta conveys a strong sense of materiality and its thinness produces, like china, an impression of lightness. The effect, described by the architects as feather-like, is at once archaic and delicate.

Throughout the long development of the design for the cladding, the architects ascribed no great importance to the view from within. This is a remarkable fact given the attention lavished on the siting and the visual impact of the building in the townscape. Indeed the progress of the design as a whole accompanied a gradual awakening to the particularities of the view. At first, the sum of Walsall in the architects' mind had been two or three monuments, a street, a canal, and little in between save ugliness and dereliction - the 'mess' designated by Pevsner. The design was born blind as it were. Only the view of the sky, it was implied, could give pleasure. In the second stage of the competition, the enclosure of the roof terrace was lowered from room to parapet height, and windows were opened throughout. Yet it was only when construction was well under way that the architects took stock of the view. The fragmented panorama of the town, now visible from the shell of the building, became in their eyes a Cézanne, a Cubist painting. Constantly changing in grain and orientation, the mostly small industrial buildings composed, to the west and to the south, a field within which a few tall multi-storey factories rose like castles.

The view is at its most eloquent in the Garman Ryan Collection, in the spaces facing toward the canal. In the room ascribed to landscapes, there is, to the right of the window, a marvellous oil sketch by Constable in which, above the darkest of grounds, the artist painted a weft of clouds, stretched, warped and distorted (like the rococo frame of the picture) to expose the bluest of skies. To the left of the window, a small Impressionist painting shows two fishermen and a dog on the grass bank of a canal, neatly juxtaposed with the real view outside: with the view which exists as well as with the view that will, could or should be.

Late in the nineteenth century, Patrick Geddes founded the Outlook Tower in Edinburgh where it still stands in the Royal Mile. Visitors entered an exhibition which explained how the local geography and the local communities formed a unified and coherent landscape. At the end of their visit, they reached the roof terrace where the view became an object lesson in the evolution of the city and its region. The New Art Gallery achieves a comparable effect, however unintentionally. Owing to the large scale of windows, thanks to the great variety of prospects and the unlikely fact that such a landscape should be offered to one's consideration at all, the views are strangely engaging and are remembered long after the memory of the Constable and the Lépine start to fade. Beautifully framed behind the glass, the seemingly demoralised landscape recovers its humanity: it is, so to speak, moralised.

A 'loose'-bodied building

In some instances, the inner frame of the window opening does not coincide with the actual glass, which reaches higher behind a bulkhead to the nearest row of external tiles. The misalignment of inner lining and outer cladding is consistent with the overall design. The architects refer to the 'loose body' of the building, within which the internal space has been carved and is 'kicking' to come in contact with the envelope in specific places. Likewise they refer to the 'loose space' of the square where specific connections are made across the townscape. Among nearby buildings, most of them greatly mismatched in scale and 'swimming at different rates', the pub which faces visitors as they walk into the square remains a rare stable element. Yet even here the stabilising axial quality has been toned down by its architects, Jonathan Sergison and Stephen Bates. The gable wall previously outlined by Caruso St John has disappeared and the roof of the pub has been given a shallow, asymmetric profile. The entrance still faces on to the square, but the pub barely encloses it - something which its modest size could not have permitted. Rather the receding plane of the roof deflects the eye skywards and sideways to the vast spaces associated with the canal. At the same time, its dark pyramidal form (suggested by the coal heap that once stood in its place) ensures that the pub retains a central position on the site.

The entire square, indeed the entire site of the gallery and the towpath running along one side of the canal, are covered with a continuous asphalt surface. The design by Richard Wentworth alternates broad, strongly contrasted black and yellow stripes. Laid parallel and at right angles to the main direction of pedestrian movement, they distort according to the variations in level of the ground. The effect is striking and weird. Walking on to the bright surface from between the stores, the eye rushes onward toward the pub and beyond while to the left, in the direction of the gallery, as the ground rises more sharply and the stripes seem broader and further apart, one's progress appears slower toward the entrance. Stepping on the asphalt from an adjoining street or building, one is made keenly aware of the ground and the space seems uncommonly vast and open, like a motorway closed to traffic for the benefit of pedestrians.

Metaphors come thick and fast to Wentworth for whom the square is in turn a pedestrian crossing, a 1950s tie, a carpet, bands left after mowing the lawn and heraldry. A further comparison, made by the artist with Princess Diana's funeral, with the particular moment when the hearse inched on to the empty motorway, is strangely apposite. From the inception of the project, Peter Jenkinson and Tim Howard, then responsible for education and culture on the local council, have argued that Walsall is not a 'fish and chips town' and that its inhabitants should be entitled to the best quality. This is arguably what they got: a square which is more dignified than the M1, provided it enters, as Wentworth

hopes, the local folklore and it remains kempt.

'Intelligent progress'

Nothing but excellence, it seems, could wake Walsall from the relative torpor in which it has sunk after one magnificent century. Dereliction on a vast scale, on land so close to the town centre stirs deep emotions and prompts a longing for beauty. While the high street remains the necessary cord uniting the building to the town, the emotional site of the gallery, the true Walsall as it were starts in Town End. For Caruso and St John, it is a Cézanne; for Wentworth, it signifies the end of the British Empire, 'sort of Russia, nothing'. To find the right emotional pitch on such a site became a major concern.

The construction of The New Art Gallery is precise and robust. Its form is powerful and unequivocal. Its siting is incomparably bold. Yet surprisingly St John describes the building as a ruin steeped in melancholy. The west façade is broadly square and appears complete, but as one approaches the gallery along the canal, aspects of it seem inexplicable, as if they had not received the proper degree of attention. Set back far behind the plane of the façade, the stainless-steel cladding at the top of the building does not seem to belong to a tower. Rather, it appears to be the back of some protrusion, possibly plant, with a window punched into it at a height that seems too low for elegance and convenience. The upper glazing of the lift shaft straddles the balustrade, as if the architects were unsure whether to wish it away or to give it a frame. Next to it, a bit of metal tries but fails to fill the gap at the corner of the building.

Contrary to the more deliberate east side, this façade betrays not a composition but several unrelated decisions. Could the building have been partly demolished and partly reconstructed? Could its windows have been fitted at different times? The bit of metal was indeed an afterthought prompted by a late request by the client. It protects the roof terrace against the prevailing wind and it is fitted with two windows. Behind it, a timber platform was installed for children who would otherwise have had no access to the view. The overall composition is undoubtely weak but it has, St John argues, the freedom, 'when looking with kind eyes', of ordinary buildings which have been modified over time. *(ill.10)*

The attitude that informs this façade, though related to Alison and Peter Smithson's notion of conglomerate order,[11] is among the most singular inventions of the architects – one with which even they are not fully comfortable, yet one which is natural to their work. Contrary to the contextual approach which still prevails, and which is exemplified by the elevations of the Sainsbury wing of London's National Gallery, it requires no mimetic acknowledgement of the surroundings. Drawing beyond what is visible into a well of emotions, it yields a finer expression. It demands empathy as well as constant material and emotional adjustments in the course of design. Sometimes intentions are formalised, for example on the east façade and inside the tower where strong expressive gestures are made. Sometimes they are muted and a more pragmatic approach dominates, for instance on the west façade and the roof terrace. When to be expressive and when to be factual are matters which are decided not by rule but by a sensitive conformation with circumstances.

Yet even the most sensitive connections between the form of a building and the local townscape will not secure a sense of belonging. The ingenious transition made by the gallery between the high street and the canal, the association with the parish church, the 'BOAK' factory and other buildings help to lock the building into a place, but they do not make it of this place. Ultimately, buildings are rooted in the institutions which they accommodate – something which Caruso St John, rare among architects, clearly

understand. No less care went into placing the building on its site than in situating its experience within the life of the town. Regional galleries are proud as well as vulnerable. The new building does not merely accommodate The New Art Gallery. By the robustness of its structure, it protects it. By the considerable prestige of its architecture, it enhances it. By the rare dignity with which it invests a municipal initiative, it enshrines it. It is a further contribution to 'the race of intelligent progress', to a complex of living institutions rooted in the working life of the town and once nourished – and with what prodigality! – by its soil.

11   Alison and Peter Smithson; *Italian Thoughts*, 1993

ill 11 Distillery, Berry Street, London. Photograph by Caruso St John

Irénée Scalbert wishes to thank the
following people who kindly gave their
time to be interviewed for this essay:

The Walsall Metropolitan
Borough Council:

Peter Jenkinson
Director of Museums and Galleries

Tim Howard
Director for Education and Cultural Sevices

Hardial Bhogal
Chief Executive

Cllr Kath Phillips
Chair of Community Services Committee

Bryan Pell
Planning Officer

With:

David Owen
Chairman of the Trustees,
The New Art Gallery Walsall

Adam Caruso
Caruso St John Architects

Peter St John
Caruso St John Architects

Colin Jackson
Ove Arup and Partners

Richard Wentworth
artist

Catherine Yass
artist

Ann French
Walsall Local History Centre

Deborah Smith
Project Curator,
smith + fowle

Jonathan Sergison
Sergison Bates Architects

David Gregory
Chartwell Land plc

David Edgar
Business Links, Walsall

The following books provided
additional material:

William Page (editor), *The Victoria History
of the County of Staffordshire*, vol. 1, 1908

W Henry Robinson, *Guide to Walsall*, 1889

A Pebble on Water

Rowan Moore

At the head of Park Street, Walsall, in a place of prominence where the Victorians planned to build a town hall, there stands a Woolworths store. It is red brick, with some stripes, a gable, an arch and a fanciful turret, as if to evoke a castle. Next to it is a Bhs of the same 1990s vintage, also red brick and turreted. The ground rises towards them, then slopes more gently as it passes through the narrow slot between to reveal a slice of sky nudged at the bottom by a shed-like pub.

Past the slot the paving gives way to broad stripes of black and beige asphalt that you have never seen in a public place before, where conventional street lights are substituted by three tall galvanised steel masts bearing lights usually used for sports stadia. You are in a ragged agora that sits relative to the two stores in the place where you might expect a car park, but whose loose planning and civic significance are distantly reminiscent of the public spaces of ancient Greece.

The space is suggested rather than defined, and seeps at its corners into the low-intensity periphery of a middle-sized Midlands working town that doesn't work as much as it would like to. To the left of the pub is a canal basin with workshops beyond, to the right a scrap of street and

a few shops. There are also the windowless flank walls of the Bhs and Woolworths. By now, however, you are aware of a far more powerful presence, the 37-metre-high tower of The New Art Gallery.

It is massive, but not overbearing. You see it in sharp perspective and its high prow is set towards you to increase its effect. It is dotted with windows which are domestic in proportion and small in relation to the whole, almost unsettlingly so. Apart from some stainless steel panels at ground level it is entirely clad in a single material, pinkish-beige terracotta tiles that diminish in size as they ascend the building and vary slightly in tone. Terracotta is highly processed mud and, while the tiles have the sharp precision of a high-tech building, they also carry with them a memory of the earth. Being tiles, they make you think of roofs, and with it the cosy thought that this potentially forbidding building is one big roof.

Being thin and looking fragile they bring delicacy to the tower, which nonetheless still appears satisfyingly solid. It manages to be many contradictory things at once, to seem hewn from a single stone, wrapped in stiff paper, and made up of many components. The next-door stores, with their bricks and arches and towers, evoke heavy masonry yet look flimsy. What you see of the gallery is its cladding of thin tiles, yet it looks solid.

The stainless steel at ground level reflects the flow of passers-by into the body of the gallery. Reflective to the tiles' matt, it dematerialises the building at the place where you would expect it to be most substantial, where in a classical building there would be heavily rusticated stones. The structure is more literally dematerialised where the corner is cut away beneath the gallery's highest point, in such a way that it would tip over towards you if invisible engineering were not tying it down. The effect, as with the cladding, is both to accentuate and undercut the tower's mass. It looks as impossible as a pebble on water.

The cut-away corner makes a porch that contains a glass lobby through which you enter a big concrete space, darker than is fashionable in contemporary architecture, and as solemn as a Romanesque church. Spaces open off it like shops off a town square, but disproportionate to the big room's scale: an education space, a library up the big flight of stairs, from where most of the light is coming, lifts, cloakrooms, a coffee bar and shop. To the side you glimpse the canal basin through subsidiary spaces, its reflective water barely lower than the reflective concrete floor inside.

Where you go next is up to you, as there is no single prescribed route. What's more, while the exterior is unified, and the detail both inside and out is consistently rectangular and plain, the interior compresses as great a variety of spaces as could be expected into the simple envelope. It is like a vertical garden or, to use the architects' favourite image, a big rambling house.

You could take the lift, one wall of which is glass, and enjoy the view of the canal pointing axially to the horizon, like the water feature of a stately home. You could go to the temporary exhibition galleries on the third floor, ample, calm, white-walled,

hard-floored spaces with light falling from clerestories above, or through the occasional window at lower level. You could go up the stairs to see the intimate works of the Garman Ryan Collection: drawings, small bronzes and oil paintings showing children, friends, informal nudes, trees, flowers and the occasional landscape. These are in two wood-lined storeys with domestic-scaled rooms opening off a double-height hall. Here the windows are all portrait-format rectangles, like the windows of an ordinary house.

Employees of the gallery might go to the second-floor offices and guests of some private function to the conference rooms on the top floor. All visitors might wish to go to the top floor restaurant, a high-ceilinged room that occupies the tower's oblong pinnacle. As they approach the restaurant from the lift or the stairhead they will see, through glass walls, an L-shaped roof terrace, beyond which is laid out the turbid townscape from which they have come.

On the lower floors they will have glimpsed pieces of this view through the gallery's windows, which reconnect the art spaces with the town outside. They may have sensed a companionship of towers, a Black Country San Gimignano made up of the tower they are in, the Edwardian town hall, and the unloved, stubby office and housing blocks of the 1960s and 1970s.

Up on the roof terrace the glimpses become a panorama of a conurbation, with large patches of building laid like cloud shadows across the land, the boundaries indeterminate between town and country, or between municipalities like Walsall, Dudley, Wolverhampton, Sandwell or Birmingham, which at ground level are well aware of their separateness. There are the masts of football grounds, pylons, mosques and churches, a humming motorway, chimneys, houses, tower blocks, hills and valleys, new building and dereliction, ugliness and beauty. But the most powerful feeling is one of connectedness. You feel that what seems disjointed at ground level now makes sense, by virtue of the journey you have just made through art and architecture and from street to roof.

The New Art Gallery Walsall opened in February 2000 to an enthusiastic response from press and public. It was widely seen as a model project of the British National Lottery: it answered a need, that of creating a proper home for The Garman Ryan Collection, while boosting a town suffering from industrial decline. It was ambitious without being hubristic, and its commissioning of architects and artists was both innovative and astute. Yet it only came about through the sustained hard work of a very few individuals, who had little or no experience of large building projects.

The gallery's director Peter Jenkinson, appointed for his skills as an arts curator and manager, had to make himself an expert in architecture, construction and politics. To raise the project's £21 million cost he had to guide it through the complexities and sometimes eccentricities of local, national and European government funding and of the National Lottery. As these sources of funding are always changing their conditions, and as the lottery was a completely new invention, there was no map for finding a way through them, just intuition and the advice of others. In the process of conceiving, developing, funding and constructing the building, it came close to disaster several times. That this confident structure now stands is due only to infectious enthusiasm, extreme dedication, political skill, luck, risk-taking and the occasional bending of rules.

The New Art Gallery's origins go back to 14 December 1891, when a special report of Walsall council's parks committee called for a municipal art gallery and museum. Such an institution opened the following year, as a single room within

the Walsall Free Library. As a building and a collection the museum remained a modest affair for several decades, attracting private donations of Wedgwood plaques; ferns and mosses; 160 specimens of birds' eggs and nests; bits, spurs and stirrups; Maundy money, some of which was later stolen; arrow heads; and souvenirs of the local heroine Sister Dora. In 1951 a presentation key and axe belonging to the late Alderman Ingram was donated, in 1954 'The Unemployed Man' by the late Gordon Herickx, valued at 70 guineas. In 1961 Miss R. Stokes gave a Cup Winners' Medal won by her grandfather as a member of the Walsall Swifts team in the Birmingham District Football Association Cup. The entire collection was valued in 1968 at £2705.

In 1973 the Walsall Museum and Art Gallery was transformed when Kathleen Garman donated her collection of art. Born in the nearby town of Wednesbury, she was the mistress and eventually second wife of Sir Jacob Epstein, and her collection was built up both during her life with Epstein and, after his death, with the American sculptor Sally Ryan. It is varied and personal, consisting of more than 350 mostly small-scale works. At its core are 43 works by Epstein himself and it is predominantly European and post-renaissance, but it also includes classical, pre-Columbian, Egyptian and other African art.

It includes paintings by Degas, Renoir, Monet, Pissarro, Bonnard and Constable, and drawings or prints by Picasso, Gauguin, Van Gogh, Cézanne, Matisse, Rembrandt, Goya and Dürer. It is also closely linked to Jacob Epstein's life, with a Modigliani drawing given to him by the artist, family portraits by Epstein himself, and a portrait of his daughter, Kitty, by her first husband Lucian Freud. There is no historic or theoretical logic to the collection beyond the personal judgement of Kathleen Garman. All the works are figurative, with a preference for portraiture, figure studies and landscapes.

George Melly called it 'marvellous' and 'extraordinary', the Daily Telegraph 'the finest personal art collection outside London to be assembled in the twentieth century', yet it was housed in an upstairs room of the public library, with no air conditioning or disabled access. During the twentieth century there were four separate attempts to build a new art gallery, but only the last was to prove successful.

In 1989 Peter Jenkinson, then aged 30, became the director of the gallery, having previously worked in museums in London and Birmingham. His primary objective was to fund and build a proper home for the Garman Ryan Collection, a task that would take him eleven years. Towards the end of this period he was working only with his assistant Micheline Clarke, and for many years he was working three hundred hours a month and without holidays, sometimes with severe effects on health. As the project developed and the gallery's team grew, others also put in long hours of hard work.

At the outset no one knew that they were embarking on such an epic. It was decided to convert a listed nineteenth-century merchant's house and an architectural competition was organised. The winners were Levitt Bernstein, a practice best known for their Royal Exchange Theatre in Manchester, who would later form the Ikon Gallery in Birmingham out of a Victorian school. £3 million towards construction was committed by the Metropolitan Borough Council. Then in late 1990 the council, its budgets under severe pressure as a result of the poll tax, decided that it could not after all afford the project.

'There was', as Peter Jenkinson now says, 'a lot of disappointment, but some key councillors, both Labour and Tory, wanted to keep it going.' He cites one in particular, the Conservative councillor Mike Bird, as 'fantastic' and, in the middle of their despondency, 'a knight rode to the rescue'.

This was Walsall's bid for money from the government's City Challenge scheme for regenerating run-down areas, under which grants were awarded to partnerships of local authorities and private enterprise. Walsall identified an area where unemployment was running at 17 per cent, with serious problems of crime and dereliction. It included Town Wharf, a run-down site at the edge of the town's main shopping area, where it was proposed to build both new shops and a home for The Garman Ryan Collection. Some saw this as too remote from the civic centre of Walsall where the old gallery was sited, but this is where The New Art Gallery would eventually be built, although its design was to change from the neo-Victorian brick polygon that appears in watercolour perspectives drawn up by the developers Chartwell Land plc.

In 1993 the bid was awarded £37.5 million, its case helped by the inclusion of the proposed gallery. Peter Jenkinson then found himself working with politicians and developers, whose culture was radically different from that of art curators. Jenkinson appreciated the efficiency with which the private sector works, but 'I saw my role as being an absolute bastard about the quality of design'. The gallery was given the site of lowest retail value, tucked away behind the planned new stores, and Chartwell appeared sceptical that it would ever happen, to the extent that they paid for paving on its site that was later removed. 'They seemed to think that Walsall was a fish-and-chip town and would always have fish-and-chip solutions', says Jenkinson. Nonetheless, the brief for the new gallery was developed with Chartwell's support, and public consultation carried out. Meanwhile two further sources of possible funding appeared, in the form of the European Regional Development Fund, which is aimed at deprived areas, and the National Lottery. First announced in 1992, and launched in 1995, the lottery was to fund cultural, sporting and charitable good causes, distributed through five bodies that included the Arts Council and the Heritage Lottery Fund. It released unheard-of sums to an arts world long starved of capital, but its cash came with stringent rules attached.

In 1994 a fundraising report was commissioned to test the feasibility of raising the £4.8 million which was then the projected budget for the new building. The report quoted authorities in the arts world who sucked their teeth and said, '£4.8 million is an awful lot of money; £1 million would be nearer the target', or, 'the proposed costs for the new art gallery are outrageous'. The report's expert authors estimated that the £400-500,000 might come from the lottery. This sage advice was politely ignored by Jenkinson. He listened instead to the Arts Council's then chairman, Lord Gowrie, who, on a visit to Walsall, advised the town's councillors to aim high, to think of a figure, in effect, and double it. Jenkinson kept pushing for the brief to be expanded, 'to the point where it became a joke'. In the end the total project cost was £21 million, of which £15.75 million came from the National Lottery.

One of the most difficult judgements facing any potential lottery project is choosing how high to aim. Too ambitious, and it falls flat on its face, with insufficient revenue and public interest to sustain it once built, as happened to lottery projects outside Doncaster and in Sheffield. Too modest, and it wastes an opportunity that may not come round again for a century. Worse, it might fail to attract the critical momentum of enthusiasm and support that it needs to happen at all.

The New Art Gallery is certainly ambitious. If the minimum requirement was to house the Garman Ryan Collection, the gallery also has a temporary exhibition floor designed for art of international calibre, extensive education areas, a library and a café. It is a building that requires the institution it contains to expand into it, and future directors and curators to match

the ambition that went into its creation. It is in part an act of faith that the art will rise to the architecture, and that the quality of the building will attract, for example, major, large scale Epstein sculptures to Walsall that have never been seen there before. Equally importantly, it would have to inspire funding bodies with the belief that its revenue costs should be supported.

It is also ambitious in its social and civic mission. The project's mission was to raise the self-esteem of Walsall and its surroundings, and to involve the widest possible public with art from every period, including the present. This involvement was to be neither patronising on the gallery's part, nor passive on the public's. 'Conventional wisdom', as it would say in the brief issued in the architectural competition, 'has it that "the Great British Public" can only cope with flower paintings or animal prints. Experience at Walsall suggests that this prejudice is profoundly mistaken. Audiences have proved far more sophisticated, more responsive and more supportive of the broad range of contemporary visual arts than journalists, critics, politicians and even some curators would often allow.'

'Access' was one of the most frequently bandied terms in 1990s cultural discussion, but the new art gallery would seek to realise it in the fullest possible way. The competition brief added that 'it is now inadequate simply to talk about audiences and their access to art but more important to talk about the interplay between and interdependence of artists, audiences, buildings and collections; an interplay and interdependence that is immensely complex and extremely difficult to establish in precisely measurable terms.' Even with the limited resources available on the gallery's old site, Peter Jenkinson and his team put on a series of unorthodox and risk-taking exhibitions designed to engage the public. Start, the country's first ever exhibition for 3- to 5-year-olds, attracted 14,000 children in ten weeks. A series of 'People's Shows' brought together local people's collections (model aeroplanes, Coca-Cola bottles, airline sick bags) and put them in the context of the gallery.

With public involvement came some controversy, and one independent Councillor was always keen to excoriate the gallery in the local papers. He, and several other correspondents, called a show on the theme of HIV 'disgusting rubbish'. However, the exhibition succeeded in its aim of raising awareness, to the extent that AIDS tests in the area rose by 30 per cent while it was on. It was also 'tried' on the national television programme The People's Verdict, where a jury of lay people voted in its favour.

Peter Jenkinson's intention was that all these qualities – ambition, civic pride, public involvement, risk-taking – were to be embodied in the new building, but finding the architects to achieve this would not be easy. British architecture was suffering from two major weaknesses, both linked to the lack of public patronage in the 1980s and early 1990s. One was that young architects had been given very little encouragement, with the result that a few famous and established practices dominated. The other was that a generation had been schooled in the values of commercial commissions, such as delivering elegant or striking buildings efficiently, rather than in the more subtle and complex cultural concerns raised by a project such as The New Art Gallery.

Clients of lottery-funded projects had to choose between a big name, who might deliver a predictable variation on their previous work, or an untried practice, with the risk that they were unequal to the task. Tough lottery rules on budget, including the requirement that lottery grants should be matched by funds from other sources, and the need to demonstrate public support militated against adventurous commissioning. The New Art Gallery, however, had important advantages. Thanks to City Challenge and European grants it had no need for matching

funding from the private sector beyond the contribution from Chartwell built into City Challenge. This allowed greater freedom in the design. And, while public consultation was conscientously carried out on the principle of building an art gallery, and while its design would have to go through the normal process of securing planning permission, no attempt was made to divine an architecture acceptable to all tastes. If this seems paternalistic it is also practical, as architecture of real quality has rarely if ever been produced by opinion poll. 'You have to respect people's expertise', as Peter Jenkinson puts it.

In March 1995, a competition to design The New Art Gallery was announced, sponsored by the developers Chartwell. It was to be in two stages, with practices initially being required to submit a portfolio of their previous work, two A1 sheets indicating their approach to the design of the new gallery, a concise report outlining their ideas and a single image summarising their submission. Up to six would be selected for the second stage, where they would be asked to develop their designs in more detail. Any qualified architect in the European Union was eligible to enter and, while previous experience was a factor, the format was also open to new ideas from untested practices. Following 157 formal registrations, 73 eligible submissions were received.

In the architectural competition as in so much else the gallery had no rule book to work to and little personal experience. Peter Jenkinson was 'an architectural virgin: I didn't know how to read plans, but through the process of the competition I became passionate about architecture.' He knew he wanted at least one senior architect on the competition jury, and an artist, and for there to be 'a mix of local accountability and national significance'. The artist would be Bill Woodrow, who as assessor on the competition for the Tate at Bankside had toured Europe's new art galleries. For the architect assessors

Jenkinson consulted Ricky Burdett, another member of the Bankside jury and then Director of the Architecture Foundation. Burdett recommended Jeremy Dixon, architect of the Royal Opera House and National Portrait Gallery extensions. Dixon accepted the invitation, and recommended David Chipperfield, whose many commissions include the masterplanning of the museum island in Berlin, and who has a sensitivity to the culture of contemporary art rare in British architecture.

As well as these professional assessors the competition brought together a foundry worker, in the person of the Walsall councillor Geoff Macmanomy, with the Mistress of the Queen's Bedchamber, the Countess of Airlie, who is also a relative of Sally Ryan and a former member of the British Rail Design Board. There was Michael Tooby, then curator of the Tate Gallery St Ives; the Mayor of Walsall, Cyril Leaker; David Carver, a member of the City Challenge board; and other councillors and officers of Walsall Metropolitan Borough Council. There was also a technical assessment panel of engineers and cost consultants.

At the first stage the discussion between these diverse assessors went on until 11 o'clock at night in a hotel at Junction 7 of the M6. Despite the potential for discord Jenkinson describes them as 'amazing, with a real shared commitment'. Six practices were shortlisted: Alsop and Störmer, Pierre d'Avoine Architects, Caruso St John, Shay Cleary Architects, Tony Fretton and muf. Of these the best-known name was Alsop and Störmer, famous for the Hôtel du Département in Marseilles. Others, including Caruso St John and muf, were included on the basis of their potential rather than their experience. It was an imaginative list notable for breaking the predictable mould of competitions for some other potential lottery projects.

At the second stage the choice came down to Tony Fretton or Caruso St John. Fretton had designed the Lisson Gallery, the most-admired and successful contemporary art space to be built in London in the 1990s. Caruso St John had built no more than some small projects that showed a special and unusual sensibility, but demonstrated a real knowledge of and passion for art, and they charmed the jury with their enthusiasm. Fretton proposed an exquisite glass box that offered flexibility. Caruso St John's design was more fixed, with a stronger civic presence. According to Jenkinson, 'their solution for housing the collection was really inspiring and they weren't snooty about the site.'

There was a long discussion, in which, for the purpose of clarifying differences, Jeremy Dixon and David Chipperfield took opposite sides. Eventually what Jenkinson calls 'the terrible moment' came, 'when they said it's your decision. I'd already made my mind up but I came out in a hot sweat. I asked if we could postpone but they said no. So I said Caruso St John.'

Adam Caruso was born in 1962 in Canada and studied at McGill University, Montreal. Peter St John, born in 1959, is English, studied at the Bartlett and the Architectural Association in London and worked for Jeremy Dixon in the early stages of the Royal Opera House project. Both worked for Florian Beigel and Arup Associates, and they set up practice together in 1990 and taught at the University of North London from 1990. At the time of the Walsall competition they were known for some competition entries and a few small projects, including houses for themselves, but had been exhibited and published and attracted critical attention for the thoughtfulness of their work.

Unlike most of their generation, they stand outside the British tradition of high-tech architecture, or the pragmatic, commercially driven modernism that grew up in the 1980s. They look more to continental architects like the Swiss Diener and Diener, Herzog & de Meuron and Peter Zumthor and, early in their career, to the Dutch Rem Koolhaas. Like these architects they base their work in the wider culture, both social and artistic, in which it is built, while stressing the importance of architectural means, such as light, material, planning and detail. They are inspired by contemporary art, without wishing to blur the boundaries between art and architecture.

Where other architects give primacy to technology, or the image of modernity, or a single style or range of materials, or abstract form-making, the consistency of Caruso St John's work is in the attitudes behind it. They have no predisposition to modern or traditional building techniques, just whatever is appropriate at a particular moment in space and time. They have an attachment to the ordinary, to the vagaries of a particular situation, while seeking to find extraordinary qualities within it. Adam Caruso's own house in London is notable as much for what he left of a crumbling old workshop as for the new architecture he added.

When the Walsall competition was advertised Caruso St John were, they say, 'getting dubious about competitions', too many of which seem set up to reach a pre-ordained result. As small young practices rarely make much money, they also had to consider whether the cost of duplicating slides and making up display panels could be justified. But they were attracted by the brief, the choice of assessors, the signs that less established architects were welcome. When they saw the drawings of the future Bhs and Woolworths stores they 'experienced a long moment of doubt', but pressed on. Peter St John went to Walsall and in 'an incredibly intense four-day period' they produced and drew a design remarkably similar to the building that now stands.

'Everything was derelict', recalls St. John, 'and it didn't look inviting', but he walked up to St Matthew's, the medieval church at the opposite end of Park Street to the site, 'and things seemed more optimistic.' It was 'a strong piece of structure in the town', and from this came the idea that the gallery should be a contemporary equivalent of the church, a marker, a fix for the town's identity. Both church and gallery are on rises in the ground that answer each other across the shallow valley that holds the centre of the town. Running against their predisposition to build horizontally, they conceived a tower. This also broke with the assumption implicit in the site's planning, that the art gallery would complete a square courtyard suggested by the side walls of the two stores.

The gallery was to be both a civic tower, like the Palazzo Vecchio in Florence, and a big house appropriate to the domestic collection it housed, where the public would be welcome. It had something about it of an Elizabethan country house, like Hardwick Hall, where 'there are amazing rooms on top and inside', and a lot about it of Adolf Loos, the early-twentieth-century Viennese architect who built mute, cubic houses, within which are compacted three-dimensional labyrinths of large and small rooms.

Externally it would form part of a loose assemblage that included the new pub, the revenue from which was an essential part of the gallery's financial planning, the existing buildings and, a remodelled canal basin, a decision that was to cause protracted discussions with British Waterways. The pub, designed by Sergison Bates, is low-lying, pitched-roofed and predominantly timber, the formal and material antithesis of the gallery tower, yet complementary and sympathetic to it. Sergison Bates have a similar outlook to Caruso St John, shunning the forced or rhetorical gesture, and preferring to let the building's structure and materials, and the intelligence of its organisation, speak for themselves. It is a place both sociable and calm, its glass walls opening it to the weather and the life of the town, its timber lining giving it warmth. Reflections bounce off the basin on to its sloping boarded ceiling, and shoppers stream past on their way to Park Street. It is informal and simple, yet it raises the spirits.

In the finished complex the whole would be bound together by the broad asphalt bands of the landscape created by the artist Richard Wentworth which, extending up the towpath of the canal, would connect the gallery with the hinterland. The breadth of the bands, combined with the bigness of the gallery, the littleness of the pub and three tall stadium lights, create a paradoxical sense of scale, both grand and intimate, and unstable and reassuring. At the time of the competition, however, all this was no more than a potential, not a worked-out proposal.

Internally, Caruso St John thought of the gallery as 'a ridiculously varied warehouse' in which a wide range of rooms – large, small, light, dark, vertical, horizontal, each proportioned to suit their use as a space for art or for children, a café or a library – were compressed into a simple exterior. 'The point was that it had many centres', says Peter St John. 'They were pushed together to make one thing but they keep their independence. We did not want a single experience that encompassed the whole, more of a field of different experiences.'

This 'warehouse' would have 'linings inside and a gauze-like outside' which translated into the solid concrete shell of the finished building, with timber and plaster in selected areas, and the thin external layer of terracotta tiles. From the outset Caruso St John took a rigorous approach to construction and detail, in which the building's structure and lining are used to define the character and scale of different parts of the building. In the completed gallery the largest and most public rooms are formed by the concrete structure, which is left exposed, whereas the small, domestic scale of the Garman Ryan galleries is created by its lining of vertical Douglas fir boards. At the same time there is an affinity between the two types of construction: the concrete floor joists are closely spaced, 'like the timber ceiling of a medieval hall', and Douglas fir shuttering was used to form the exposed concrete walls, leaving board marks whose rhythm and pattern echo those of the timber lining.

Thus the constructional logic of the building – its need for a primary structure, a cladding to keep the rain off, and linings to conceal its electrical, ventilating and other services – becomes the means by which the different 'experiences' that Peter St John talks of are created. There is a mutually reinforcing tension here between the austerity of the means, heightened by the limited range of finishes and a hard won consistency of detail, and the richness of the effects.

Both inside and out, although a forceful and distinctive structure, the gallery does not attempt to be complete in itself. It is rather something that it is completed by the art it exhibits, by its visitors and its context, and by the commissioned art such as Richard Wentworth's landscape and Catherine Yass's photographic images projected in a giant window by the entrance during the launch. Despite its powerful presence, it sits easily within its variegated surroundings. It does not outsmart its neighbours with glamour, or 'show them up', as Peter St John puts it, but includes them in a collective enhancement of the town. 'This idea that it makes Walsall new was never articulated', says Adam Caruso, 'but maybe it is one of the most significant consequences of the project.'

The first time Peter St John and Adam Caruso met Peter Jenkinson was when they delivered the model for the second stage of the competition. They thought him 'a bit young and slightly crazed'. After winning they took him to see some of their inspirations, the work of Herzog and de Meuron and Diener and Diener in Basel, and gave him a "concrete tour" of London, in order to demonstrate the many forms the material can take. A relationship of mutual respect and understanding rapidly developed between client and architect. Such an understanding would be needed.

An intense year followed the announcement of the competition result in October 1995. In order to receive a grant from the European Regional Development Fund a building contract had to be in place by the end of 1996 and a price agreed with contractors, an arbitrary rule that was to cause serious trouble. In the course of these twelve months the design was to be developed, further public consultation to be carried out, a lottery bid submitted complete with business plan and other supporting documents, funding secured, the building's engineering and details worked out and specified, and tenders from contractors sought, received and evaluated.

The architects, engineers and client team went to the Lousiana Museum near Copenhagen to study the light levels of its successful exhibition galleries, and to Kettle's Yard in Cambridge, which like the Garman Ryan houses a domestically scaled collection of twentieth-century art. There they established that floors in Douglas fir worked well with such a collection. They went to Tate St Ives to talk to Michael Tooby and met Peter Wilson, the Tate Gallery's director of buildings. From them they learnt technical, back-of-house requirements, 'what to do and what not to do'.

Caruso St John took part in a two-day public consultation workshop, and the proposals were exhibited next to the escalators in the town's main shopping centre. Further workshops were carried out with the gallery's staff, and the results of both exercises were fed into the brief.

While the overall concept of the design changed little, some significant changes were made. The biggest was placing the temporary exhibition galleries above the Garman Ryan Collection rather than below, as they had been in the competition design, as the client felt it was preferable for the visitor first to experience the permanently accessible collection, rather than the temporary galleries which would be closed between exhibitions. The elevations took a long time to design. A proposal to silkscreen images of Epstein's work on to them was dropped and much work went into the choice of materials and the detail of the windows to achieve the desired effect of giving the glass and the terracotta cladding equal visual weight. To avoid excessive monotony the tiles were to be made in five shades, mixed into a random pattern.

The engineers Ove Arup worked out how exactly the building's overhanging corner could be achieved, where structure is removed at precisely the point where it is most needed, and how to tie the building down so that it wouldn't tip over. A further challenge was the fact that the concrete was exposed, and had to be constructed in 7-metre-high sections at one time. The complexity of the resulting reinforcement in the concrete walls meant that any changes to window positions had major structural implications, and working it all out was only possible with three-dimensional computer analysis. Meanwhile the cost consultants Hanscomb had to monitor and control the building's budget, and in autumn 1996 the project managers Bucknall Austin (now Citex) were appointed. Their job, according to Bucknall Austin's Simon Whelan, 'was to be a technical friend to a client who knew what they wanted, but had no idea how to get it. We had to deliver a building that met their aspirations.'

Before the lottery bid was submitted Peter Jenkinson had to negotiate a further political hurdle. The project was eligible for support from two different distributors of lottery money, the Arts Council and, because it involved works of historic importance, the Heritage Lottery Fund. That there is such a split between the two bodies reflects, in Peter Jenkinson's view, 'a stupid British distinction between old and new culture', but at a late stage the Arts Council advised him that it would be diplomatic to put in a bid to the HLF, as in the early stages of the lottery the two bodies had not defined the boundary between their responsibilities.

Jenkinson was certain that he didn't want the project jointly funded by two bodies, as contacts at the Tate Liverpool, where this had happened, had warned him of the resulting delays and arguments about who should pay for what. He knew that he wanted to be supported by the Arts Council, who had indicated that they viewed The New Art Gallery as a model project, by which the lottery would be remembered. He also knew that the gallery would need funding for its running costs once open, and that the Arts Council would be more inclined to contribute to these if it had funded the capital costs which, in the end, was exactly what happened. Jenkinson therefore conducted 'a huge battle of talking quietly but vigorously to people on committees.' Spotting and negotiating these obstacles was once again a question of nous and the advice of others, not working to any established rules.

Jenkinson had to argue with quantity surveyors for the Government Office of the West Midlands, who said the building cost too much per square foot. 'We said, too much compared to what? To retail? To offices? Or to other galleries internationally?' The Arts Council's architectural assessors also gave them an unexpectedly difficult two-and-a-half hours, apparently disconcerted by the design's failure to conform to the established canons of high-tech architecture. It lacked, for example, a soaring atrium. 'All of us were in our mid-30s', says Jenkinson, 'and they seemed to see us as these toddlers. They kept

saying "show us the route through". and Peter and Adam kept saying, "the whole point is that there is no single route. You can eat your pudding first if you like. You can explore."'

Eventually a presentation was made to the Arts Council's lottery board. The film producer David Puttnam, a member of the board, was supportive, but a question was posed on which the whole project, and with it the years of work of conceiving it, building a team, running the competition and developing the design, could have foundered. The chief executive of Walsall was asked whether the Council would, if necessary, underwrite any shortfall in the gallery's revenue budget. A no would have been disastrous. He said yes.

After an agonising wait the Arts Council announced that they were awarding £15.75 million to the project. The deadlines were met for tendering and ERDF funding of £4.5 million was secured. A firm of contractors, Sir Robert McAlpine, were appointed. McAlpine were not the lowest tenderer, but their price was competitive and the gallery team felt they showed the best understanding of the building and would be the best to work with. Work started on site in January 1997, with completion of the construction scheduled for December 1998. The project, however, was still to come close to catastrophe.

In February McAlpine found rock in the ground, which delayed construction of the basement by two weeks. During the summer they had difficulties erecting the complex concrete structure, and by December they were claiming for a 20-week extension to the contract, with associated additional costs. A windy and wet winter caused further delay and in February 1998 McAlpine indicated that they would be making further claims for delay. A savings review was carried out to avert the threat of the project going over budget but within a month it was apparent that the capital budget was likely to be exceeded.

In the summer the failure to complete the structure on time was having a knock-on effect on the cladding contractors and other trades and in August McAlpine claimed for costs of £1.7 million over the original budget, which were contested by the gallery's consultants. At this point lawyers were consulted by both contractors and clients, and discussions held with QCs in London. By January 1999 the relationship between contractors and designers was at its most antagonistic and, on the advice of the project managers Bucknall Austin, independent reviews were carried out to establish what had gone wrong. In April McAlpine were predicting a completion date of late August, eight months later than the original date, and claiming for extra costs of more than £3 million.

McAlpine argued that the problems stemmed from inexperienced architects with an inadequate knowledge of the construction process. Caruso St John believe that McAlpine failed to understand the building properly at the outset and organise themselves accordingly. Simon Whelan, the project manager, broadly supports the architects' view, while suggesting that their commitment to quality sometimes made them too inflexible in dealing with problems. All would agree that a major source of difficulty was the rush caused by the ERDF's deadline. In order to meet it prices were sought from contractors when a large amount of the work was not yet fully detailed and specified, which created ample room for doubt and disagreement.

Simon Whelan, whose job was to manage the warring project impartially, also criticises the Arts Council's policies. They favour traditional forms of building contract, which give architects a high level of influence, but which also carry a higher level of risk of overspend than more modern, contractor-led contracts. Yet they do not bear this risk themselves, refusing to consider applications for further grants when things go wrong. The Arts Council also reduced at the start the contingency sum Whelan believed would be necessary. 'They have got to take a hard stance on money', he says 'but they fiddle with projects without taking the responsibility.' Peter Jenkinson also observes that, where Walsall was flatly refused extra cash, some high-profile London lottery projects, such as the Royal Court Theatre and, notoriously, the Millennium Dome, were bailed out of their difficulties.

Late, and possibly 25 per cent over its construction budget, the project was in danger of being what Whelan calls 'a disaster for Walsall, a disaster for the Arts Council, a disaster for everyone.' While a few luxuries, such as independently operated electric blinds, could be omitted, seriously compromising the quality was not an option. 'If we had delivered averageness', he says, 'you can easily imagine what the press would have said. We would have wasted £21 million and four years of effort.'

While Whelan was adjudicating the rights and wrongs of the case, and lawyers were being consulted, frantic efforts were made to find a peaceful solution and stay out of the courts. McAlpine's main board in London was approached and the chairman of the Gallery's Development Trust, David Owen, pursued his contacts with McAlpine. The project, says Whelan, 'was one or two meetings away from going completely pear-shaped when we got both sides to pull back.' In May 1999 a figure of £592,000 was agreed over the original contract sum in settlement of the McAlpine claim for over almost £4 million. Construction was eventually completed in August, to be followed by fitting out and installation of the exhibits.

That projects like The New Art Gallery happen at all is extraordinary. That major disasters are averted along the way is a miracle. That they also manage to be ambitious, imaginative and pioneering, and to sustain to completion the ideals with which they started is almost a defiance of the laws of nature.

The success of Walsall is due to a huge number of people: the Victorian worthies who conceived the first gallery, Kathleen Garman and Sally Ryan, the officers of Walsall's council, councillors of all parties, the gallery's staff, trustees and consultants, the competition assessors, the architects, project managers, engineers, quantity surveyors, artists, landscape architects and other experts, the Arts Council's officers and assessors, the builders, the Walsall public who offered their opinions and support, the press, the friends of the project who gave their advice and experience.

All these people had to be enthused. As Peter Jenkinson says, 'proselytising is a huge part of the project. No one who has got involved has done so half-heartedly.' What he doesn't say this support has been generated by his own passion, energy, infectious enthusiasm and personal and political skills, his ability to spot rocks and reefs in the uncharted waters of public funding. People are converted by his openness and sincerity, his lack of a hidden agenda, his transparent desire to involve others. Adam Caruso says, 'he is like a boulder rolling down hill. He gets everyone involved.'

Even now, the future success of the gallery is not certain. It could indeed prove too ambitious, funding might dry up, a lacklustre future director might fail to rise to the job, visitor numbers might tail off, the world of art and museums might regard Walsall as too remote to favour with their interest and support, no matter how good the building. No public project worth having comes without the risk of failure. But the reward for risk is achieving something as extraordinary as The New Art Gallery Walsall.

A different perspective

Kate Fowle
smith + fowle

When The New Art Gallery opened, thousands of people ventured to see inside. As visitors made their way through the exhibitions their experiences were regularly punctuated with panoramas of Walsall and beyond. It was the first public building in the town to offer aerial views and fresh perspectives on the borough.

Over the next four months, even after gallery opening hours, passers-by continued to see Walsall in a new light. Each night, images of local people and places emerged from the 10-metre expanse of glass on the Window Box, which Caruso St John designed as the gallery shopfront. Pausing to watch, viewers momentarily found their reflection absorbed by projections of the community and environment they were a part of.

Town:Walsall was a temporary installation by Catherine Yass, produced specifically to be seen from the Window Box from dusk to dawn. Working in response to the architects' desire for the building to have a reciprocal relationship with the town, Yass found different ways to reveal previously unnoticed aspects of Walsall. Over three years the artist shot footage from a helicopter and in the underground sewers, as well as filming people at work and play in locations such as a fish and chip shop, tattoo parlour and boxing club,

capturing people's fleeting gestures or expressions. Fourteen sequences were converted to DVD, with the colour saturation and speed of the footage manipulated to create what could be seen as shimmering photographs. Yass explains the motivation for the piece as wanting to 'place something moving underneath this very substantial building, as if to tickle its underbelly.'

While Yass explored the space of the Window Box as a potential interface between the town and gallery, Richard Wentworth was working on the design and materials for The Gallery Square. In a letter to Peter Jenkinson, he used photographs to question how the building relates to and re-defines its location: 'Can indoors move outdoors and vice versa? Are we archaeologists? How do we recognise the material we encounter? Is everyone a sign, or only some?' This thought process resulted in a pedestrian area made by contrasting a light-coloured Zebraflex with black asphalt to form 6-metre-wide stripes. These travel relentlessly over the contours of the site and down the canal path, uniting the disparate geometry of the spaces. From street level the design for the square signifies that people have taken over from vehicles. When viewed from the gallery windows, the bands take on that pristine quality

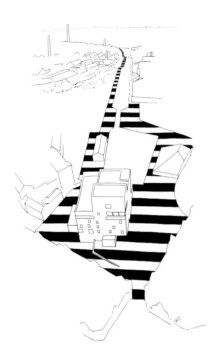

associated with immaculately mowed lawns.

The visual simplicity of The Gallery Square reflects the confidence of the building. Wentworth describes his approach as 'bold, unapologetic and plain speaking', which is also a fitting description of the way Yass used the Window Box. By day it was empty, effectively displaying the raw fabric of the building in the gallery shop-front. At night the projections focused attention on a new perspective of the town, echoing what the views from the building offered.

Both commissions reveal how the artists and architects found a collective language in their ambition to unite the practical and phenomenological aspects of the building. Shared sensibilities and assured personal visions made for intelligent dialogues between art and architecture, which in turn stand as testimony to the powerful relationship between the different practices.

As work on The New Art Gallery gathered momentum, three artists were given commissions that related to the construction process. Each recognised how the whole project had grown out of peoples' aspirations for Walsall, developing through individuals investing time and energy to make the dream a reality. Ming de Nasty was invited to make photographic portraits of those responsible for creating the building, from the scaffolders to the plumbers, the structural engineers to the administrative staff, recording the otherwise anonymous contributions in perpetuity. Gary Kirkham developed a visual archive that captured physical evidence of life on site and the internal structures that are now concealed. Anne Parouty worked with a team to produce a website that provided contextual information to the background of the Gallery and the subsequent developments. Aimed at architecture students and information-hungry onlookers internationally, the site included time-lapse footage of the growing building, as well as interviews

with Peter Jenkinson and Caruso St John on their ambitions for the designs.

An early statement made by Caruso St John outlines how they 'are interested in urbanism that responds to real situations (that is) to do with spaces of democracy and difference, and with the inherently loose and broken character of English urban fabric.' The 'real situation' of The New Art Gallery project, as part of a larger and much needed regeneration programme, was one with broad social and cultural implications, particularly for those who lived or worked in Walsall. There was an injection of capital and optimism into the Borough as a result of the desire to house art. This provided the motivation for the art project programme *to be continued>*, which extended the gallery's intervention into the town. In the year running up to the opening, more than twenty artists from the UK and abroad were invited to spend time in Walsall, visiting the Gallery as it was under construction and exploring the town. Each artist then developed a new work in response to these first-hand experiences, creating temporary interventions into existing infrastructures from July 1999. Some were inspired by particular sites or buildings, others by aspects of Walsall's history or through dialogues with local people. Together the commissions offered different ways of engaging with Walsall's culture and built environment.

After learning of the burgeoning pork-scratching industry, Anthony Key created a pork-scratching collection for the Local History Museum, which was contributed to by many of the manufacturers. The Highgate and Walsall Brewery collaborated with Gary Kirkham to make the first beer mats for their ten pubs in the area. Alan Kane added to the selection of free walking tours of Walsall, producing *Walsall for Adventurers*, which encouraged readers to re-evaluate their relationships with routines and familiar places. In it he invited people to consider themselves 'as a potential collaborator in adventures as

Design for The Gallery Square,
project by Richard Wentworth

yet unconsidered', reflecting the whole ethos of The New Art Gallery project. Local shops put purchases into carrier bags designed by Mark Harris, Ming de Nasty and Jeremy Deller, so shoppers participated in making a mobile exhibition as they moved through the streets. Performance artist Bobby Baker set up a café in the middle of a shopping centre, offering free tea, hand-made biscuits and chat to those who wanted to stop and rest. Henrik Plenge Jakobsen visited Walsall from Copenhagen to produce his first commission in the UK. Picking up on the feelings of change in the town, and indeed the country, he painted the word ANGST against a psychedelic pink background on to the side of the Age Concern building, opposite the social security office. A year later the mural remained untouched by the local graffiti experts. Fiona Banner installed a large neon sign stating *Be there Saturday sweetheart* at the top of the tallest office block. Sitting high above the corporate insignia in the town centre and visible for miles around, the piece offered an enigmatic proposition to those who saw it. The text was an extract from one of Jacob Epstein's love letters to Kathleen Garman, which Banner discovered in the Garman Ryan Collection. She saw the work as a celebration of the passion and collaboration that made The New Art Gallery what it is today.

The artists' commissions produced throughout the development of The New Art Gallery gave voice to a diversity of art practice and its relevance to everyday situations and places. When the first gallery opened in Walsall in 1891 it had the ambition to ensure that 'the manners of the people will become softer and less uncouth'. We have moved on from this paternalistic stance, recognising the possibilities for art to mediate social and cultural exchange and returning to a belief in the potential for art to shift perspectives and expand ways of thinking. Just as artists have always worked with their own experiences and

interpretation of a situation or subject, so can the audience. The New Art Gallery is a reflection of this way of thinking, creating a space that embraces democracy and difference, where people and places, fantasies and realities can fuse.

Fiona Banner -
*Be there Saturday
sweetheart*, 1999
Henrik Plenge Jakobsen -
Angst, 1999

Bobby Baker -
performance, 1999
Ming de Nasty -
carrier bag, 1999

Art

Dear Peter

Richard Wentworth

Dear Peter,
      The world is made of light.
Thousands of paintings & photographs
emphasize and celebrate it. The two
Josef Albers photographs of the road
were made in 1930. The top view is to
the north, the bottom looks south, this
much we can say.

Are we archaeologists? How do
we recognise the materials we encounter?
Is every one a sign, or only some?

How do light & shade change
what we think? Can a warning be
precious? Granite punctuated with
marble. Provincial town, where people
know their masonry.

Do people seek light and shade
for different reasons?
Is it different for different people?

If the world is made of light,
what is the ground made of?
What impression do we make on it?
Should we leave one behind?

Paved with gold?
Made of end grain timber, certainly.

When we say 'landscape', what
ever do we mean? Can it be too
beautiful? (Safe to say this looks
northwards, in the northern hemisphere)

Can indoors move outdoors, and
vice-versa?

Can warnings be decorative?
Can decoration be a warning?
Why is paint different from
something made of itself? Is wet
different from dry?

What is a palimpsest? Is this
one? Dug, rolled, scraped, painted.

Is decoration measurement?
Is measurement decoration?
Light measured by shade.

It depends on your point of view,
the time of day, the time of year.

yours
Richard

Town: Walsall

Catherine Yass

town: bakery
town: ceiling
town: fish & chips (eat in)
town: pub
town: tattoo

town: boxing
town: cell
town: helicopter
town: sewer
town: temple

town: cafe
town: fish & chips
town: kebab
town: skipping

Portraits
Ming de Nasty

Allen Drummond
Works manager

Helen Rathgay
Engineer

Dave Robinson
Crane driver

John McKeogh
Carpenter

John McKee
Concrete finisher

Lee de Vall
Scaffolder

K. Perry
Boardmarker

Karl Brocklesby
Tile fitter

Mick Gubbin
Steelfixer

Sean O'Connor
CODE

Neil Dumphy
Window fitter

Paul de Vall
Scaffolder

Wayne Halligan
Labourer

Building Construction
Gary Kirkham

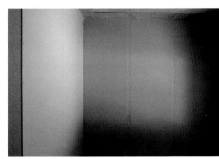

Using the
Building

Drawings

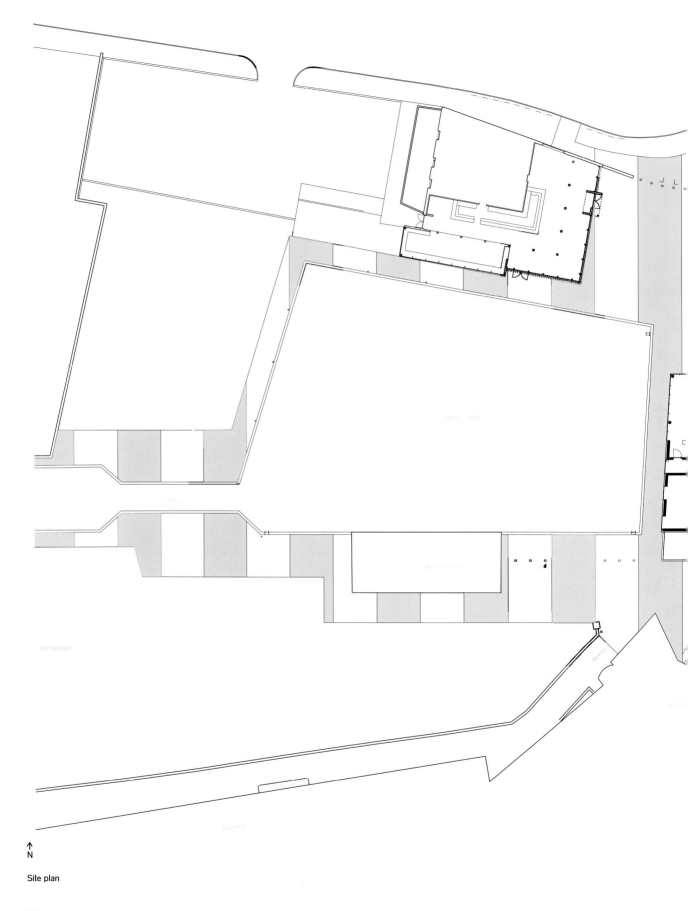

↑
N

Site plan

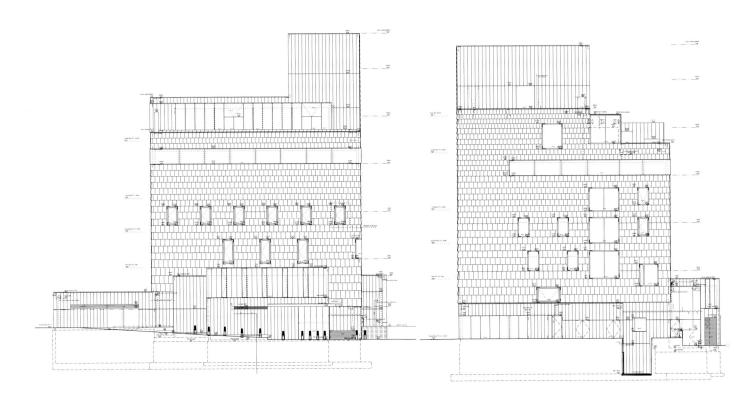

0   10

Elevation south   Elevation west

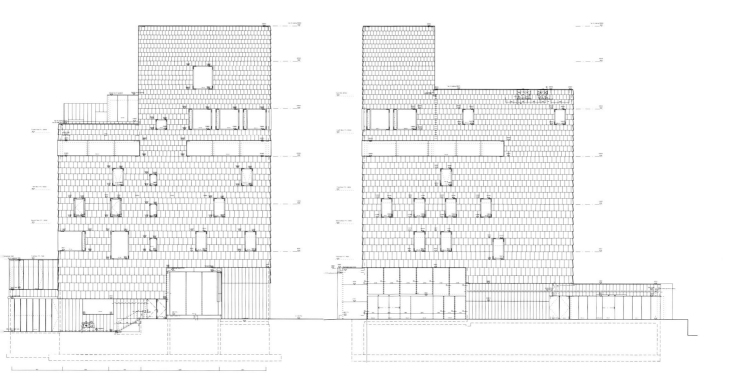

ation east

Elevation north

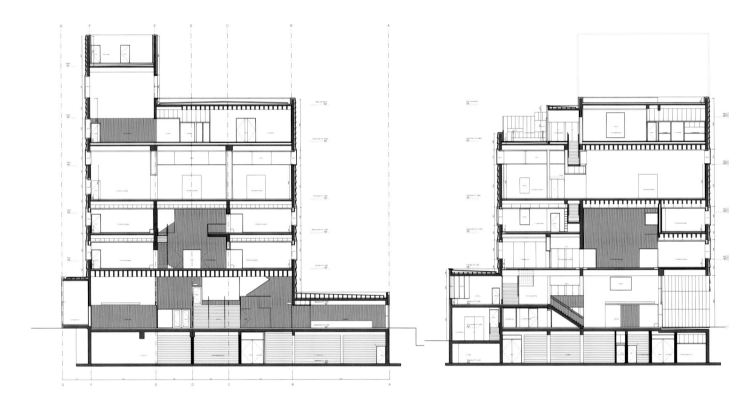

Section A-A

Section B-B

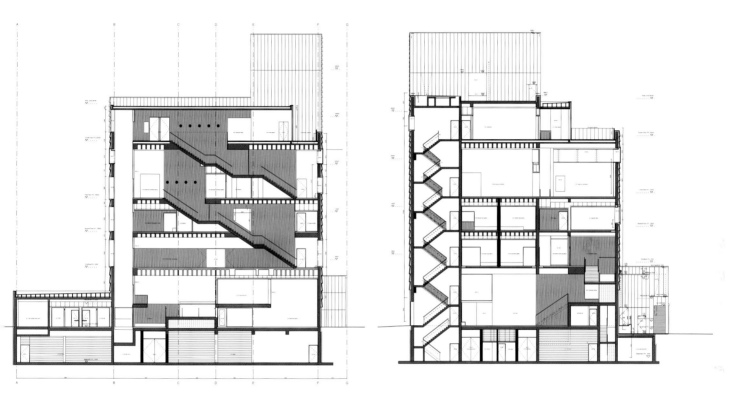

Section C–C

Section D–D

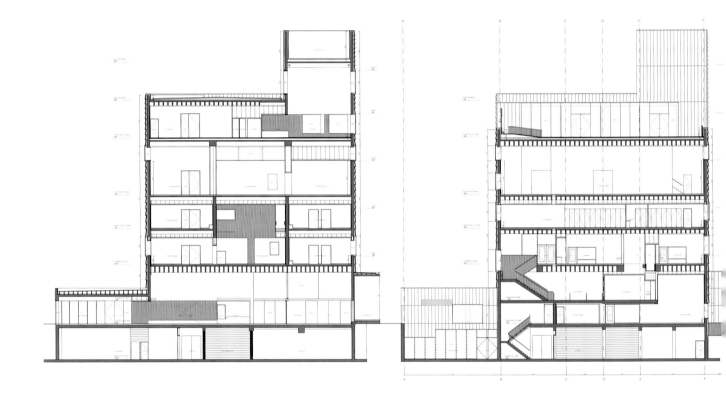

Section E-E

Section F-F

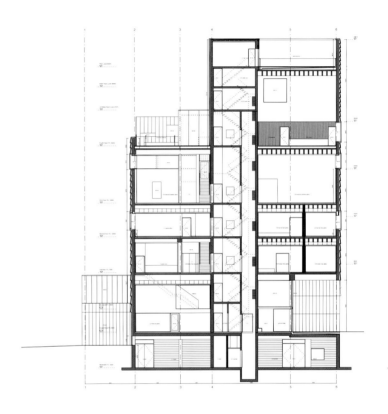

Section G-G

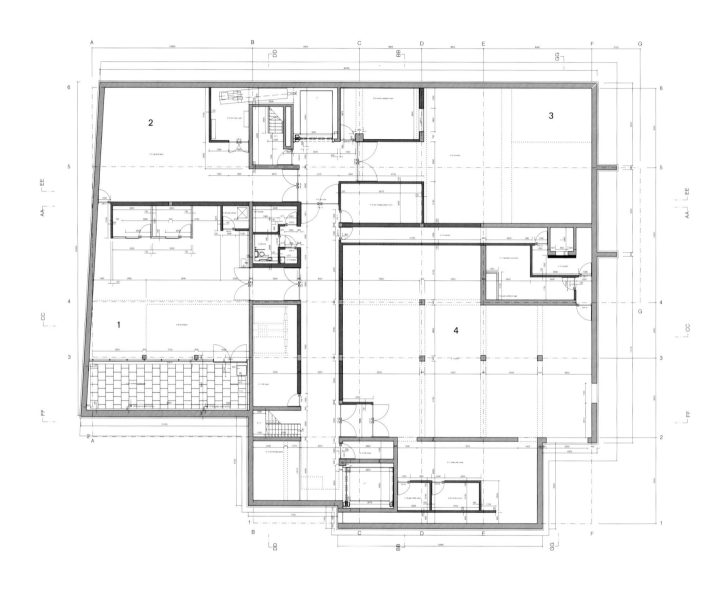

Basement plan
1 Workshop
2 Store
3 Art store
4 Plant

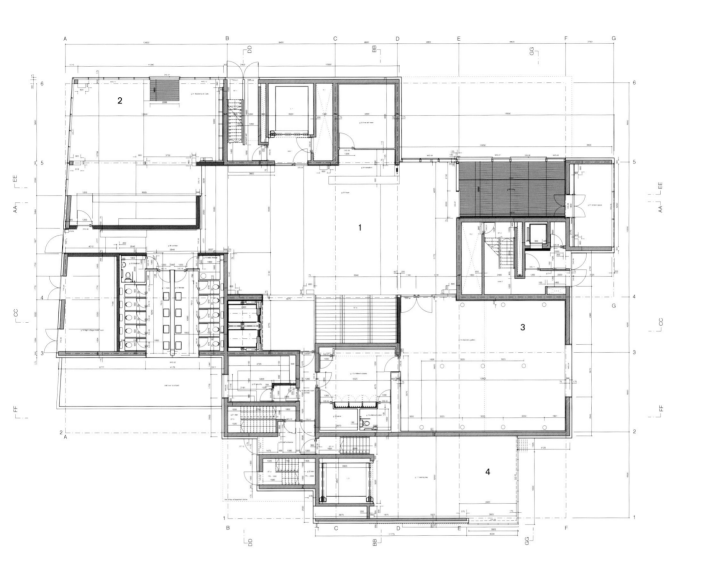

Ground-floor plan
1 Entrance foyer
2 Shop/café
3 Discovery Gallery
4 Loading

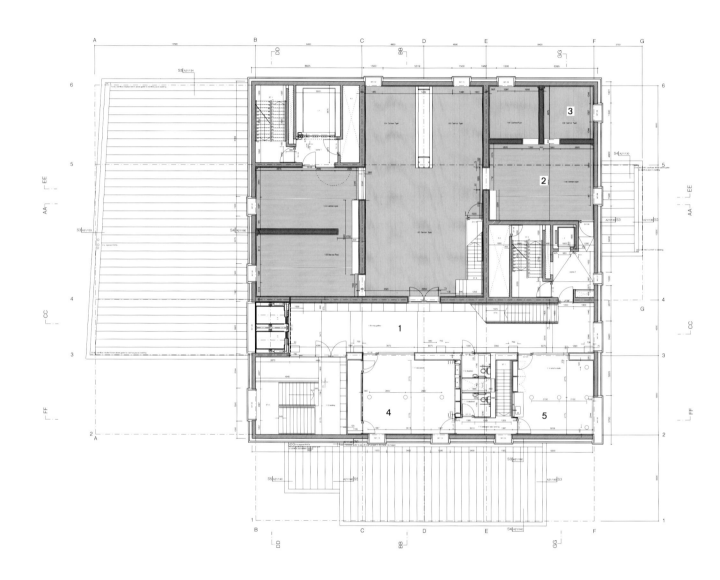

1st-floor plan
1   Long gallery
2   Garman Ryan hall
3   Garman Ryan galleries
4   Education room
5   Artist's studio

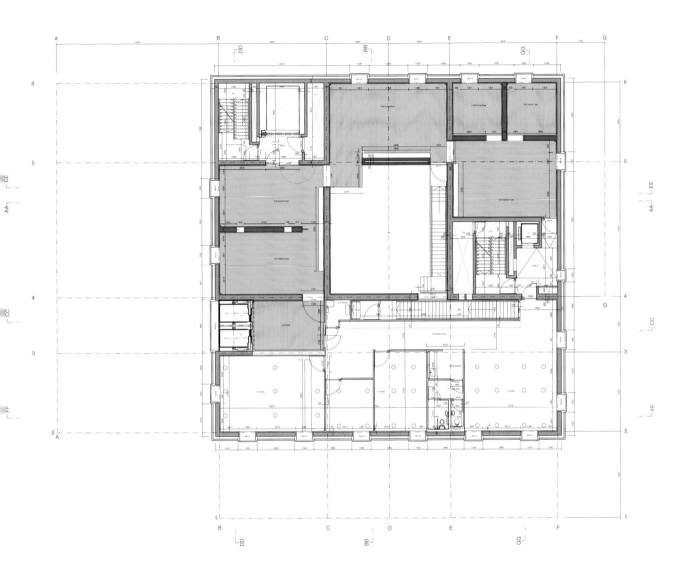

2nd-floor plan

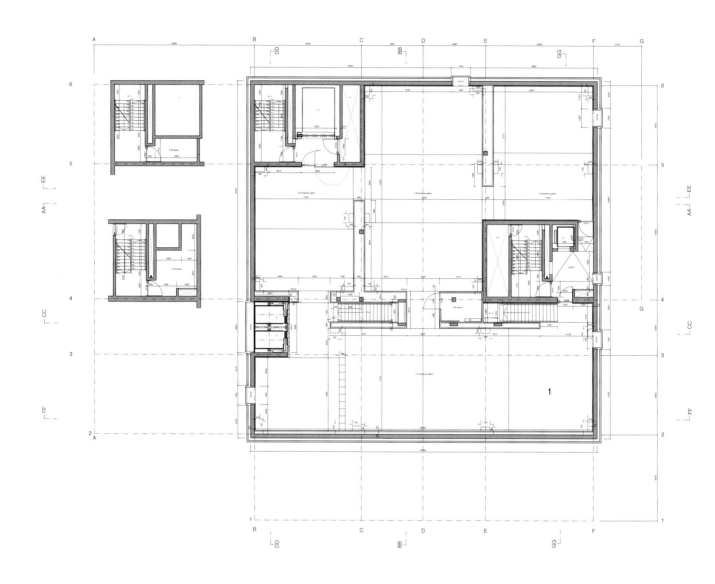

3rd-floor plan
1 Temporary exhibition galleries

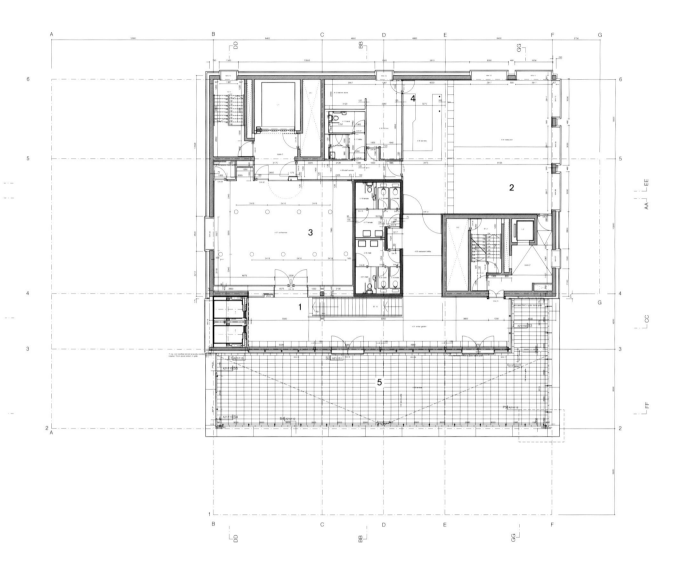

4th-floor plan
1 Winter garden
2 Restaurant
3 Conference room
4 Kitchen
5 Terrace

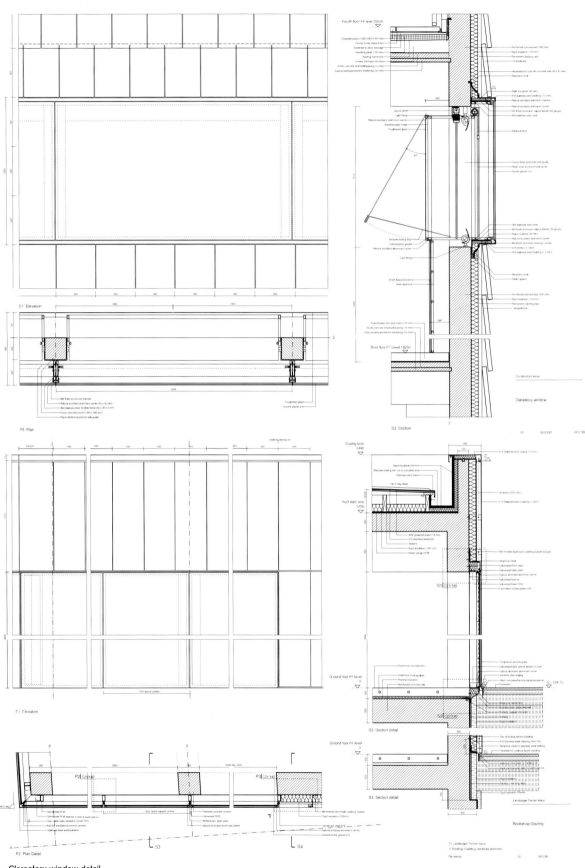

Clerestory window detail
Bookshop cladding detail

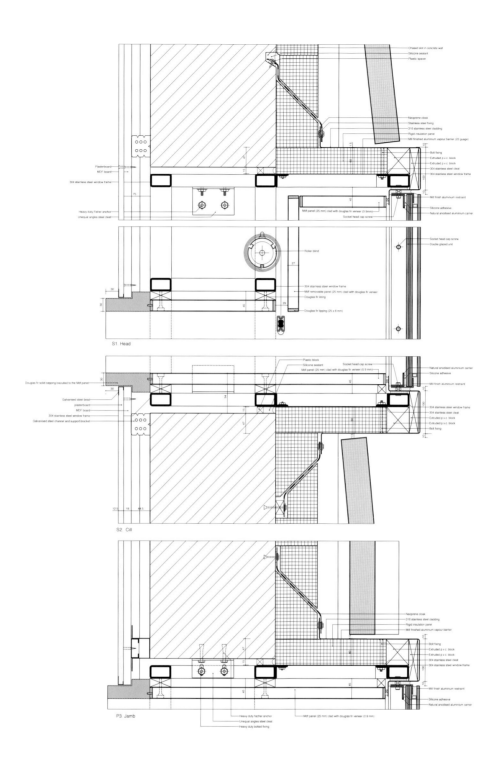

Garman Ryan Collection, window details

Photographs 2
Hélène Binet

We would like to thank our capital funders:

Walsall Metropolitan Borough Council
The Arts Council of England
The Arts Lottery Fund
West Midlands Arts
The European Regional Development Fund
Walsall City Challenge

The New Art Gallery Walsall would like
to thank the following Epstein Patrons
for their generous contribution:

The Owen Family Trust

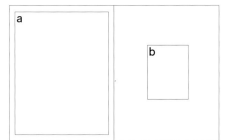

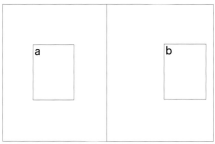

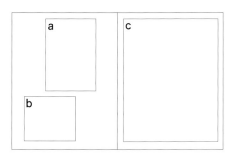

Pages 116 + 117

a b
View along canal from west

Pages 118 + 119

a Lock-keeper's cottage
and west elevation
b View from north

Pages 120 + 121

a Detail of east elevation
b Gallery Square with The Wharf pub
c The Window Box (Town: Walsall,
by Catherine Yass)

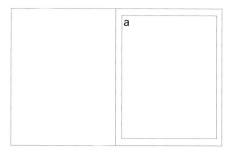

Pages 122 + 123

a Entrance foyer

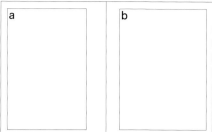

Pages 124 + 125

a b
Garman Ryan Gallery

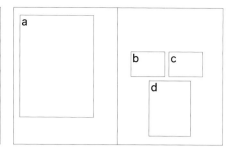

Pages 126 + 127

a Third-floor, temporary exhibition gallery
b c
Fourth-floor, winter garden
d Fourth floor, restaurant

Reference

Bibliography

'Caruso St John,
Walsall Art Gallery',
a+u, April 1994

Michael Ratcliffe,
'Alchemy of the
Black Country arts',
The Observer, 12 November 1995

'Strange New World',
Blueprint, December 1995

Paul Finch,
'A substantial gallery
with a domestic scale',
The Architects' Journal, 18 January 1996

Jonathan Glancey,
'They're so Modern',
The Independent, 26 March 1996

Lee Mallett,
'The Strong Silent Type',
Building Design, 9 August 1996

Adam Caruso,
'Byggande/Kultur',
arkitektur, March 1997

Caruso St John Architects,
Work, 1997

M Stuhlmacher,
'The physiognomy of a doll's
house, The New Art Gallery
Walsall by Caruso St John',
OASE 47, 1997

Adam Caruso,
'Shell, Cladding, Lining',
OASE 47, 1997

Peter Allison,
'The Presence of Construction:
Walsall Art Gallery by
Caruso St John',
AA Files 35, spring 1998

Ian Latham,
'The Wharf in Walsall',
Architecture Today 86, March 1998

Ellis Woodman,
'Build my gallery high',
Independent on Sunday, 31 May 1998

'Walsall Art Gallery',
a+u, April 1999

Irénée Scalbert,
'Caruso St John and the Art of
Action Building',
a+u, April 1999

'Walsall Art Gallery',
Lotus International 102, 1999

Hal Ingberg,
'Sampling and remixing an
architecture of resistance,
Canadian Architect, September 1999

'Caruso St John Architects,
Walsall Art Gallery',
Lotus, September 1999

Peter Buchanan,
'Caruso St John in Walsall',
Architecture Today, November 1999

Brian Carter,
'Competitive Edge',
Azure, November/December 1999

Giles Worsley,
'The new kings of the castle',
The Daily Telegraph, 29 January 2000

Thomas Kai Keller,
'Realistisches Spiel
mit Gefuehlswelten',
Neue Zürcher Zeitung, 3 March 2000

Giles Reid,
'Character Building:
Caruso St John in Walsall',
Monument, April/May 2000

Irénée Scalbert,
'Caruso St John, Galerie
d'Art Moderne, Walsall,
Grande Bretagne',
le Moniteur Architecture amc, May 2000

Adam Caruso,
'La Tyrannie de la Nouveauté',
le Moniteur Architecture amc, May 2000

Brian Carter,
'Solid Citizen',
The Architectural Review, May 2000

Irina Davidovici,
'Huis voor de Kunst',
de Architect, June 2000

Kaye Geipel,
'Nordwestlich von Birmingham',
Bauwelt, 16 June 2000

Peter Allison,
'Gallery Square in Walsall',
Baumeister, August 2000

Jeremy Melvin,
Young British Architects,
Birkhäuser Verlag, Basel 2000

Peter Allison (curator),
Outside in, London Architecture,
Verlag Anton Pustet, Salzburg 2000

Caruso St John Architects,
Arquitecturas de Author 13, T6 ediciones,
Pamplona 2000

Hubertus Adam,
'Eins Plus Eins ist Drei',
Archithese 3.01, 2001

Penny McGuire,
'Walsall Gallery',
Architectural Record 05, 16 June 2001

Caruso St John,
*New Trends of Architecture in
Europe and Japan 2001*,
Shinkenchiku – Sha Co., Tokyo 2001

Vicky Richardson,
New Vernacular Architecture,
Laurence King Publishing, London 2001

Dorota Lesniak,
'Galeria Powszechna',
Architektura & Biznes 114, 2002

People

Architect
Caruso St John
Martin Bradley
Adam Caruso
Laurie Hallows
Rod Heyes
Alun Jones
Peter St John
Andrés Martinez
Silvia Ullmayer

Project manager
Citex
Simon Whelan

Quantity surveyor
Hanscomb
Michele du Saire
Jonathan Harper

Structural engineer
Ove Arup & Partners
Simon Hancock
Lidia Johnson
Andrew Sedgewick

Façade consultant
Arup Façade Engineering

Acoustic consultant
Arup Accoustics

Planning supervisor
Ove Arup & Partners

Access
David Bonnett Architects

Contractor
Sir Robert McAlpine Ltd
Clive Huntley

Art handling
Bruce McAllister

Security
Andy Baskeyfield
David Young

Landscape architect
Kinnear Landscape Architects

Discovery Gallery design
Ben Kelly Associates

Graphic design
Michael Nash Associates + JANE
Jane Chipchase
Anthony Michael
Stephanie Nash

Artists
Ming de Nasty
Gary Kirkham
Anne Parouty with Sakab Bashir and Mark Ball
Richard Wentworth
Catherine Yass

Photographs
Hélène Binet

135

A CIP record for this book is available
from the British Library

First published 2002 by
B T Batsford A member of Chrysalis Books plc

Chrysalis Books plc
64 Brewery Road
London N7 9NT

Project editor Deborah Smith
Designed by Michael Nash
Associates + JANE
Art project photography by Peter Barker/
Ravi Deepres
Drawing on page 73 by Quintin Lake

Printed and bound in China

ISBN 0 7134 8787 9